KNOWLEDGE, VALUE AND EDUCATION
An Axionoetic Analysis

KNOWLEDGE, VALUE AND EDUCATION

AN AXIONOETIC ANALYSIS

S. R. BHATT

WITH A FOREWORD
BY
SHRI KIREET JOSHI
SPECIAL SECRETARY
DEPARTMENT OF EDUCATION
MINISTRY OF HUMAN RESOURCE DEVELOPMENT
GOVERNMENT OF INDIA
NEW DELHI

GYAN PUBLISHING HOUSE
NEW DELHI-110002

KNOWLEDGE, VALUE AND EDUCATION

AN AXIONOETIC ANALYSIS

ISBN : 9788121200608

Reprint in 2016 in India by
Gyan Publishing House
5 , Main Ansari Road, Daryaganj,
New Delhi - 110002
Phone : 9811692060

E-mail : books@gyanbooks.com
gyanbook@vsnl.com
Website: gyanbooks.com

To My Parents
Who Made Me What I Am

FOREWORD

THE PRESENT WORK presents a study of the theory and practice of education in relation to knowledge and values from a philosophical standpoint. The underlying assumption of this work is that philosophy can and should provide a basic justification of the discipline of education.

Education and life are inter-related. The aim of education cannot be different from the aim of life, since education is an attempt to organize life itself. It is through the scrupulous examination of the natural processes of life that one can arrive at the basic principles of education. In a certain sense, life itself is the best teacher of life, and one can trust life to arrive at the knowledge of principles and processes by which the aims of life can increasingly be realised. For this reason, it takes centuries and millennia to fathom into the profundities of life and discover the principles by which the art and science of life can be developed. Considering this inter-relationship between education and the life, it can be said that while life is spontaneous, education is a deliberate process, and in the totality of existence, both the spontaneity of life and deliberateness of education are interlinked. Basically what education attempts is to ensure an *accelerated* process of the growth and development of life. Again, education must ensure a *right rhythm* of acceleration. This implies a process of determination of the aim of life, the rate of rapidity with which the aim of life can be realised, and the variation that should occur in the rate of rapidity in relation to various stages of development. It will be obvious that education is, thus, an extremely difficult endeavour, and there is a need to examine the principles and functions of education on a continuous basis. This shows a direct relevance of educational philosophy.

In recent times, there has been a long debate on the theme of values. One of the prevalent views is that values are subjective and that each individual should be left free to pursue values as he subjectively views them. According to another view, which is equally prevalent, values are only emotional reactions to situations, and they do not have any direct relationship with the realm of knowledge. In the ultimate analysis, both these views tend to belittle the importance of the pursuit of values. On the other hand, there is today an increasing awareness of a crisis through which mankind is passing at the present juncture of human history. It is being increasingly acknowledged that this crisis is basically due to the fact that while man has advanced a great deal in certain directions, his progress in regard to psychological, aesthetic, ethical and spiritual domains has been arrested. The basic cause of the crisis is, it is said, disequillibrium between the internal and external life of man. This analysis of the present situation brings out the importance of the pursuit of the internal life, the prominent aspect of which is related to values. Are values eternal ? Can we know eternal values, if there are such ? Do values change from age to age ? Are there two categories of values, those which are eternal and those which change from time to time ? If so, what are the criteria by which they can be distinguished from each other ? These and allied questions seem to be extremely important, and a serious consideration of these questions is urgently required, particularly when education is being increasingly called upon the task of building up the defences of peace in the minds of men and of bringing about a radical change in human nature.

It is, therefore, gratifying that Professor Bhatt has undertaken a sustained exercise to examine the question of the problem of values and their place both in education and in life. As one reads the pages of this book, one finds that this exercise is rigorous, impartial and objective. And the result of this exercise is not only stimulating but also instructive.

The present work offers an axionoetic approach to education. It will be seen that this approach attempts to bridge the realm of knowledge and the realm of values. In the present climate of philosophical thought where interdisciplinarity is being increasingly emphasised, the approach of Professor Bhatt's book will be found to be highly pertinent.

In India, we have just adopted a new policy on education. If one reads the policy document, one finds an underlying persistence of emphasis on value-oriented education. It speaks of the all-round development of personality as the basic objective of education. It underscores the necessity of pursuing national unity and national integration. It proposes to encourage those values which are distinctive in Indian culture. It is evident that as a sequel to this policy document, there is bound to be a multi-faceted exploration of the entire realm of values, and this exploration will necessarily demand a philosophical examination of the relationship between education and values. In that context, too, Professor Bhatt's work will be found to be opportune.

I have no doubt that this book will provide both to the scholar and to the common person some of the basic materials that are needed for initiating an enquiry into the *raison d'être* of education. It will also provide to those who are in charge of developing educational policy of the country, the requisite guidance about the underlying assumptions of value-education. I am sure that readers will be benefited if they consent to undertake the exercise which this book is bound to stimulate.

July 4, 1986
Department of Education
Ministry of Human Resource Development
Government of India
New Delhi

KIREET JOSHI

PREFACE

THE PRESENT MONOGRAPH is based on a well-grounded assumption that philosophy can and should provide a foundation to the discipline of education and that no system of education can be meaningful unless it is based on the solid footing of a systematic philosophical reflection. Though it has too often been declared that education is the dynamic side of philosophy or an active aspect of the philosophical belief, no sincere attempt has been made to provide a genuinely philosophical basis to education. Of the various philosophical dimensions of education like ontological, ethical, axiological, logical, epistemological etc., the last two have been left untouched by our educational thinkers and researchers, and the treatment of the first three dimensions has been more or less fragmentary and comparatively superficial.

This prevailing circumstance has motivated me to take up the epistemic aspect of education because it is epistemology which constitutes the stepping stone to philosophy. The avowed task of this work, therefore, is to establish the correlation between knowledge and education. Knowledge plays a fundamental role in the sphere of education. It is the very stock, so to say, in the trade of education. And that is why a theory of knowledge is quite basic to any theory of education.

I am extremely grateful to Shri Kireet Joshi, Special Secretary, Ministry of Education, for sparing his valuable time to write a foreword to this monograph. He has been an ardent champion of value-orientation in education and therefore it is in the fitness of academic requirement that this monograph should carry a foreword from him.

I am also thankful to Mr. J. L. Gupta of M/s Gian Publishing House for bringing out this monograph.

Head, Deptt. of Philosophy S. R. BHATT
University of Delhi
Delhi-110007

CONTENTS

CHAPTER

1

INTRODUCTION

0.1 IT HAS BEEN SAID about the Hegelean philospohy that it died of being misunderstood. The same has been the case with general philosophy as well. So much has it been misconceived, mistrusted and misused that the word 'philosophy' is more often than not used contemptuously to brand anything that is vague, confusing and abstruse. To a great extent the so-called philosophers and the teachers of philosophy are responsible for this plight of philosophy. Therefore, before we embark upon our avowed task of establishing the correlation between knowledge and education, we shall do well to see the exact nature and function of philosophy, education and philosophy of education.

1.0 WHAT IS PHILOSOPHY?

Etymologically, philosophy means love of wisdom but functionally it means both the seeking of wisdom (process) and the wisdom sought (product). This wisdom it must be made clear, is in no way mere abstract ratiocination. It really means practical orientation and vision (for use in life) based on pure knowledge. Philosophy, thus, stands both for the theoretical knowledge of the nature of life and its conditions, and the practical (applied) knowledge of the principles of conduct for the practical guidance of life. It is a systematic reflection over the entire reality with a view to fathom its mysteries. Human life is the most important facet of the reality and therefore it is one of the most important tasks of philosophy to solve the riddles of human life and existence.

These days under the impact of empiricism and scienticism an attempt has been made by some philosophers to restrict the scope and function of philosophy to mere linguistic analysis. Undoubtedly such an analysis has its own importance to clear the rubbish from the path of philosophical thinking but that is not the end-all and be-all of philosophy. That is just the preliminary task. Philosophy has to do something deeper and more serious. It has to address itself to the imminent problems facing the mankind, failing which it would cease to be the 'Queen' of all the disciplines.

Against this background we can formulate three important tasks of philosophy viz.,

(*i*) to study the nature and phenomenology of our knowledge, and to formulate the norms and criteria of its validity and truth.

(*ii*) to ascertain in the light and by the means of the instruments and equipment so developed, the nature of the reality—within (human life), without (external world) and above (supramundane Reality).

(*iii*) and, finally, in the light and on the basis of the enlightenment so gathered, to develop and formulate, for life's guidance, the goals or values and the ways of life.

1.1 What is Education?

Education is a deliberate conscious process which consists in a modification of the natural development of man. Man is imperfect by nature. His life is a process of development which tends towards something which is more perfect. This results in the modification of his behaviour pattern. In order that this modification may not fall short of its goal, it must be well engineered. This presupposes an adequate formulation of beliefs and aspirations of human existence which, in other words, are called as aims or objectives of education.

Education, moreover, is a medium through which the society transmits its heritage of past experiences and modifications, system of values and the modes or skill of acquiring it.

Thus, all education is a means for the betterment of human life. It is the fruitful utilisation of the knowledge attained by the mankind for the enhancement of human existence.

1.2 Philosophy and Education

Every philosopher, if he is to make his philosophy of any worth, must determine what his philosophising implies for the process of education, because to know is to be (i.e. knowledge for the sake of being) and in order to be education is the only means which is proper and adequate. History of mankind testifies the fact that all the great educators were also great philsophers, and their philosophical views were inevitably reflected in their educational schemes.

Since education is an instrument for the betterment of life, all educational questions in their ultimate analysis rest on the philosophy of Life. Although not very many of the modern educationists attempt for a precise formulation of their philosophy of life, none can afford to miss it. As it has been said, there can be no alternative between philosophy and no philosophy but only between a good philosophy and a bad philosophy.

If the dependence of education on philosophy is that inevitable then why to feel shy of it, why not to admit it from the front instead of pushing it in from the back?

The modern estrangement between philosophy and education has been unfortunate for both. Such of those modern educationists who tend to rely on empirical sciences at the despise of philosophy need only be reminded of what Spencer had said that true education is practicable only to a true philosopher, or what Gentile had warned that the belief that men may continue to educate without concerning themselves with the subtle problems of philosophy means a failure to understand the precise nature of education. Similarly present day 'philosophy-men', specially the Analists, who betray the restricted view of the sphere of philosophy, should also be told that Plato and Hume, Russell and Whitehead etc. from whom they have derived inspiration, did not regard education as a study unworthy of philosophical consideration.

1.3 What can Philosophy Contribute to Education

If the general philosophy is a systematic reflection over the entire life to understand its nature then educational philosophy is also a systematic reflection comprehending the phenomenon of education in its entirety. Every system of education has to base itself on certain ends and policies, and it is the business of philosophy to provide these ends and policies to education. The framing-up and selection of the educational ends and policies presuppose value-considerations and value-judgements. The science of education because of its positive nature cannot make normative decisions. Hence is the need of a philosophical framework.

All the major issues of education are, at bottom, philosophical. We cannot examine the existing educational ideals and policies, or suggest new ones, without considering such general philosophical problems as the nature of the good life to which the education should lead; of man himself, because it is men we are educating; of society because education is a social process; and of the ultimate structure of reality which all knowledge seeks to penetrate.

Philosophy is helpful to education in three important ways ;

(*i*) in providing theories of the nature of man, society and the world ;

(*ii*) in suggesting the ends and means of the system of education ;

(*iii*) and, in examining the rationality of our educational ideals, their consistency with other ideals and the part played in them by wishful or unexamined thinking; in testing the logic of our concepts and their adequacy in explaining the facts they seek to explain, and in demostrating the inconsistencies among our theories and indicating the precise range of the theories that are left when the inconsistencies are removed.

1.4 Philosophical Foundations of Education

Every system of education must have its footing on the solid basis of a systematic reflection about the nature of reality (sat), knowledge (cit) and values (ānanda). Of the three philosophical foundations of education, viz., ontological (pertaining to sat), epistemic (pertaining to cit) and axiological (pertaining to ānanda), it is the epistemic which is the most fundamental and therefore the foremost in importance. This is because, though Reality has existential priority, it is knowledge which has noetic priority. That is, in order that there be knowledge at all, there must be a prior being of Reality. But in the noetic process knowledge reveals Reality and thus acquires priority. Therefore, from a human point of view the approach to Reality is only through knowledge and there is no passage from Reality to knowledge. As regards value it rather constitutes the very culmination of the process of existence and knowledge, and thus comes at the end.

2.0 Facets of the noetic basis of Education

Knowledge plays a fundamental role in the sphere of education. It is the very stock, so to say, in the trade of education. And that is why a theory of knowledge is quite basic to any theory of education. The epistemic inquiry helps to evaluate the educational thoughts and practices, develops them and thus enables us to use them as instruments of human progress. One of the important functions of education is the acquisition and imparting of knowledge, but before we undertake this teaching-learning process, it is desirable to know the nature and sources of knowledge itself so as to get an insight into the complexities and intra-connections of its diverse forms and facets. This would not only help us in maintaining proportion and perspective in curriculum but would also enable us to avoid the superficial and get at the essential. Further, education is a purposive activity, devoted to the development of individual's personality. Its direction and shape are determined by human beliefs, aspirations, aims and ideals, which in turn are based on and moulded by knowledge. Education thus is determined in structure, contents, range etc. by the varied forms of knowledge and their heirarchical inter-relations, and therefore no theory, and for that matter the practice also, of education can be complete and enduring if it is devoid of its noetic foundation. We may now discuss in brief some of the broad areas where epistemology provides a basis to education

2.1 Knowledge, Values and Education

Philosophy, and epistemology for that matter, is concerned, among other things, with the problem of value. This is because philosophy attempts to study Reality keeping human being in the focus. The quest after values, and the attainment thereof, constitute the very core of human life. There is an innate necessity for man, caused by his finitude and imperfection, to participate in the process of value-realisation. Now all questions about values (not of values) are basically epistemological. For example, what is the nature and the source of values? What kind of existence do they have? How can they be acquired? etc. are the questions which presuppose the capacity of human mind to know values. All these questions are equally relevant to education. For example, if it is said that it is only by effort that one can know and realise a value, this is just the same as to say that experiences which educate are fundamental to value-realisation. A way of looking at value epistemologically necessarily needs to look to educative activities as means for their realisation.

From the above it is quite evident that the process of value-realisation is basically an educational one. There is an educational dimension indigenous to axiology and reciprocally there is a necessary connection between educational objectives and value-seeking. The process of education tends to refer to a set of values or ideals embodied and expressed in the objectives for which knowledge is imparted. That is why the questions as to what is man and what he aspires for, are the unavoidable preamble to any kind of education, formal or informal.

2.2 Nature of Knowledge and Education

The problem of nature of knowledge has occasioned a severe controversy in the field of epistemology. Different schools of thought, starting with different metaphysical assumptions have taken different positions and have offered different answers for this. These various epistemic approaches have greatly influenced and moulded the thought and practice of education. They have reflected themselves in similar corresponding shades in the sphere of education. For example if knowing is identified with doing, as a pragmatist or instrumentalist would do, its natural consequence in the field of education would be a stress upon activity methods, like projects, experiments, problem-solving etc. The only genuine knowledge would be knowledge-in-action. The possession of a body of certified knowledge would be at a discount. The past heritage may be doubted and discarded. The contemplative and meditative sides of education, quiet enjoyment of literary and artistic pursuits etc. would tend to be regarded as waste of time. Knowledge by description would be neglected and emphasis would be laid on knowledge by acquaintance.

Instead, like a realist, if knowing is regarded as rèpresenting something which is there outside to be known, then education would be regarded as a medium of revealing the outer reality to the knower. Learning would be regarded as true and effective if pupil's impressions correspond to outer reality. The learner would be regarded as a passive instrument, having an empty mind, a *tabula rasa*, as Locke would put it, when he would start the process of knowing. Through curriculum only that knowledge would be imparted which was already known to the teacher and the text-book writer. All new invensions would tend to be regarded as mere discoveries. More emphasis would be laid on natural sciences and knowledge of the external world. Religion, spirituality and disciplines based on introspection etc. would be put to disuse. Knowledge by description would not be discarded, but, on the contrary, established traditions would be banked upon as an idealist would do, then emphasis would be laid on the constructive activity of the mind out of what is given in immediate experience. Knowledge would not be regarded as *about existence* but as existence itself (Brahma id bhavati brahma). The pupil would be regarded as 'in the process of becoming' and education as the means to the fullest efflorescence of the potentialities of man lying hidden in him. Education would be a constant training of body, will and mind. It would consist of not mere study of books etc. but of active participation in, personal identification with and real embodiment of what is known. In the learning process self-activity, introspection, meditation etc. will acquire prominence. As against the traditional formal and naturalistic education of the realist there would be greater freedom for imaginative insight. Spiritual education would occupy a place of honour in the curriculum.

Further, if by knowledge we mean only that which is stated either orally or in writing then such a view would certainly put a premium upon verbal examinations. If by knowledge we mean that which is useful in adjustment, then, like the pragmatist, practical efficiency and experiments would be relied upon. If by knowledge we mean inner experience which is ineffable, as a mystic or intuitionist would contend, then the consequences of such a view would be that written examinations would be put at a discount.

Now a little reflection over the metaphysical assumptions with which these schools start, would make it clear that they do not use the word 'knowing' in one and the same sense, and hence is the diversity in their positions. The pragmatist uses the word 'knowing' in the sense of that activity, mental or physical, which helps the man in his struggle for existence with a hostile environment. The realist however, uses the word 'knowing' in the sense of the mental process which enables a man to mirror the external reality with which he has to get himself adjusted for the advancement of life. An idealist, on the other hand, uses the world 'knowing' in an altogether different sense Since he does not believe in any outer reality friendly or otherwise, for him all knowing is 'self-knowledge' only and it consists in being aware of one's own 'Being'. This analysis clearly suggests that there is no antagonism in the diverse positions adopted by these schools and they can be regarded as complementary. They refer to different phases of life and reality and therefore in a particular context each one is true. This conclusion would certainly have a tremendous effect in the field of education since the educators are very often led to think that these schools are quite incompatible and educational implications of one school can never be compatible with the educational implications of the remaining schools. Such a fallacy of exclusiveness can be brought to the notice of the educationists only through the analysis of the epistemological positions of the so-called conflicting schools.

2.3 Sources of Knowledge and Education

With regard to the sources of genuine knowledge, again, there has been no unanimity among the philosophers. Different thinkers, having different background and assumptions have emphasised different sources like sense perception, reason, intuition, revelation, authority, existence etc. These differences resulting in characteristic positions have reflected themselves heavily in the planning of educational activities and programmes. For example, an empiricist who discards all a-priori knowledge and accepts only the a-posteriori, would place an exclusive weightage on science and would fawn upon philosophy and cognate rational disciplines. A rationalist, on the contrary, would bank upon a-priori knowledge. He would discard all empirical studies as superfluous and would harp upon purely theoretical and intellectual pursuits. A pragmatist, again, would go to another direction and accept only those disciplines which are based on immediate experience and which are helpful to the individual in promoting and furthering his life and existence. He would emphasise vocational and practical education.

Here, again, a calm and serious reflection would help us to realise the fact that diverse are the facets of reality and hence diverse are the ways to know it. Consequently none of the recognised sources of knowledge is false or complete. In the all-enveloping gamut of knowledge each finds its adequate place and hence none should be discarded. Such a synthetic vision would have a tremendous impact in the sphere of education and would help to remove all false dichotomies.

2.4 The Validation of Knowledge and Education

One of the major tasks of education is to acquaint the pupil with the true criterion of knowledge. That education cannot be regarded of any worth and sense which does not enable a man to discern what is right, good and useful. No education can be perfect and complete if it merely concerns itself with bare acquisition of knowledge without inculcating the ability to test its validity. The optimum development of personality, which has been the recognised aim of education, requires the cultivation of a reasonably adequate pattern of judgement, and this can be provided only by imparting the definite criterion of meaning and truth. This is what is called the education for critical faculty. This has been the nature of education in ancient India.

Different criteria for truth have been advocated in different schools of thought. At the philosophical level preference for one or other of the criterion has been usually made in different schools under different metaphysical and epistemological assumptions. But in actual practice most of us are likely to use all the criteria usually proposed, with the emphasise shifting from one context to another. In daily affairs in which our beliefs are concerned with the objects, qualities and relations that can be perceived we tend to accept the criterion of correspondence. On the other hand, when we are concerned with formal problems, dealing with conceptual relations, we tend to rely on a coherence test of truth. Instead, if we are concerned about the truth or desirability of complicated practical judgements, socio-political arrangements, we tend to use a pragmatist test judging the consequences of action in terms of the more or less well-established norms or values of a culture. In the field of education such a position would result in the synthesis of the triple tests of truth. This would widen the scope of curricula.

2.5 Knowledge and Curriculum

Knowledge plays a tremendously important role in the framing up of the curriculum and the scheme of school organization. The curriculum being the only avenue of approach to knowledge it behaves us to understand the nature of knowledge. Knowledge is the very essence or the soul of the curriculum. A curriculum design or pattern is distinguished by the way in which it embodies knowledge. Therefore before any framing up of curriculum can proceed, the curriculum framer must fully acquaint himself not only with the nature, sources and criteria of knowledge but also with the heirarchical organization and priorities of disciplines with regard to their teaching through the curriculum.

In the light of the above analysis of the problem pertaining to this area, we can examine the various traditional forms of curricula and by an evaluation of their points of strength and weaknesses we may evolve another form which may suit the growing needs of the country. The problem of explosion of knowledge can also be solved by discerning the essential from the superficial. Here we may put forth the following criterion for the discernment, viz., 'what would be desirable for every man as a man to know?' and the answer to this may provide us with the guideline for the formulation of the curriculum.

2.6 Knowledge and Teaching-Learning Strategy

Since the aim of all education is to impart knowledge successfully; the success of the teaching-learning strategy lies in properly knocking at the door of knowledge. The curriculum is the store, as it were, in which all knowledge is locked up. The teaching-learning dynamics is the key to open up the lock and to lay open the stored knowledge. This can be made possible only when the key is suitable to its purpose. This not only brings teaching-learning strategy nearer to knowledge, but also makes that process dependent on knowledge.

Different approaches to the nature of knowing and learning and their relationship would tend to make a difference in the nature of teaching-learning process. For example, a pragmatist would want an active school, an active pupil and an activity-oriented programme. The function of the teacher would be not to impart theoretical knowledge, but to organise, select and direct experiences so that the participation in the activities may bring the maximum knowledge to the pupil. The interest of the pupil would be heavily relied on and it will be the responsibility of the teacher to stimulate, arouse and direct the interest of the pupil. The pupils would not be asked to be engaged in fruitless memorisation but will be taught to think through the problems. A realist, on the contrary, would stress on the attainment of the knowledge of precise relationships between two facts, events or objects. Learning would be regarded as conformity to what is outwardly true. The mind of the pupil would be repeatedly impressed with the nature of the external things. Drill, memorisation of the well-established information, careful observation and constant checking of facts, etc. would be some of the means of moulding the understanding to conform to what is objectively so. An idealist, on the other hand, would insist that education must conform to the supreme ideal of mankind viz., fellowship with the Ultimate Reality. Here the teacher would be given a place of position and importance. Interest, effort, discipline, self-study, self-education, freedom of will etc. will be main features of learning process. The idealist would not make the pupil a devotee of any one particular method, but rather would like him to be a creater of method.

The above consideration would lead us to one important conclusion, viz., knowledge is the end and the teaching-learning process is the means to acquire it. No means can be successful in the acquisition of its avowed end unless it is in conformity to its end. So it is the nature of knowledge which would determine, or from which would follow, the shape of teaching-learning strategy.

In India at present we are experimenting with regard to the suitable and congenial form of teaching-learning strategy. But unless we are clear with regard to the nature of knowledge we have to impart and also with regard to the curriculum which we have to evolve and frame, it would be quite futile and pointless to labour in experimenting upon the precise form of teaching-learning strategy. As a matter of fact such a thing would naturally come as a consequence or corollary of the curriculum.

3.0 The upshot of the foregoing considerations is that from every angle of the educational problems there comes a demand for a noetic-basis of education. The art of education will never attain complete clearness in itself without this basis.

CHAPTER

2

NATURE AND SOURCES OF KNOWLEDGE AND EDUCATION

THE NATURE AND SOURCES of knowledge have always been problematic to the mankind. There has never been unanimity among the thinkers with regard to the precise nature of knowledge, because they look at it from a specific angle and whatever vision they get from it that alone is regarded as genuine knowledge. Some look at it as something abstracted from life and as having an exclusive unrelated existence. Others maintain that knowledge is dependent on life-experience and is subservient to them. It is nothing more than an instrument for the betterment of life. Some identify knowledge with the pure cognition of the 'Faculty-Psychologists' and deny its scope upto conation, whereas there are others who vigorously champion that conation is the very essence of knowledge. Some people advocate various levels or even kinds of knowledge, one sublating the other.

Though usually a two fold categorical distinction is maintained between valid knowledge (pramā) and invalid knowledge (apramā), some Realistic thinkers do not accept any genuine invalidity in knowledge. According to them that which is referred to as invalid knowledge is in reality only a partially valid knowledge, an incomplete knowledge. All knowledge is essentially true only (Yathārtham sarvam vijnañām). However, no one denies the fact that all knowledge is not necessarily complete and hence true. This leads to the problem of determining the ways which may provide complete knowledge. With regard to the sources of knowledge also the same differences of opinion prevail which are witnessed regarding the nature of knowledge. According to the Indian epistemologists there are six ways of knowing, to wit, pratyakṣa, anumāna, śabda, upamāna, arthāpatti and anupalabdhi. Of these the first three are fundamental ways and the last three can be brought under the head 'anumāna'. In the western epistemology we find a similar classification which is as follows: sense-experience (c. f. pratyakṣa), reason (c. f. anumāna), authority (c. f. śabda), intuition (a special type of perception) etc.

Since knowledge is the stock displayed in the curriculum and disseminated through educative process, the differences of opinion with regard to the nature and sources of knowledge reflect heavily in the field of education as well. That is why different theories of knowledge also have correspondingly different theories of education. Here we shall undertake a brief survey of their respective positions.

0.1 Idealism in Epistemology and Education

Within idealism different philosophers have developed different theories of knowledge. But the basic position of all idealistic thinkers is that since reality is a whole, the knowledge which reflects reality is not fragmented but unified. Any piece of knowledge becomes significant only to the extent that it is seen in its total context. Hence all ideas and theories must be validated according to their coherence within a continuously developing unified system of knowledge.

Since man is regarded as an active agent that analyses and synthesises any event or object that he encounters, the idealists believe that the purpose of teaching is not so much to familiarise the student with a mass of information as to stimulate him to discover the meaning of this information for himself. Since what is known depends in part upon the knower, the student must relate his information to his own previous experiences, so that what he learns, becomes significant to him personally. Learning, therefore, does not consist of absorbing selected items of knowledge, but of personally exploring the reality that is around and within us.

2.0 Realism in Epistemology and Education

According to the realistic epistemology the object known exists independently of the knower. It is external to the knower and is not affected by the knowing process. Mind does not create the world but merely receives information from it or copies the world. For a realist an idea is true if it corresponds with the reality it represents.

Since we merely discover reality and do not create it, the pupil must be given the knowledge of what the world actually is through the teaching of positive sciences. The child cannot be given any freedom to find out for himself what he wants to know, since what he wants to know may not be what he should know. The initiative in education, therefore, lies with the teacher. It is his responsibility to decide which knowledge the child should learn. Though the interest of the pupil should not be neglected but at the same time it should not be the sole consideration. The main criterion should be the validity of knowledge in terms of correspondance.

2.1 Pragmatism in Epistemology and Education

As against the realist, the pragmatist conceives of the mind as active and exploratory rather than as passive and receptive. Man does not simply receive knowledge but makes it. Knowledge does not lie in mere revelation of the reality but it is a product of the transaction between man and his environment.

According to the pragmatist, knowledge is acquired by locating and solving problems. The teacher, therefore, should construct learning situations around particular problems which he regards as truly significant for his pupils. Instead of teaching traditional subjects, he should prepare the pupils to confront the life-situations and life-problems and to enable him to understand the environment in a better way. The pupil's interest and curiosity should be the main motivators of learning. Instead of spoon-feeding, the pupil should be allowed to learn himself. The teacher should merely assist and guide him when he is in difficulty.

2.2 Perrenialism in Epistemology and Education

In the field of epistemology perrenialism has no distinct existence yet its tendencies are discernible in some idealists and realists. According to this trend of thought human nature and the reality as a whole are changeless. Accordingly, knowledge too is everywhere the same. Had it not been so, people would not have sit together and agreed upon anything. To acquire knowledge is the essence of education. Since knowledge is everywhere the same education should be everywhere the same. Since man's distinctive characteristic is his ability to reason, education should concentrate on developing the rational faculty. Pupils should be taught certain basic subjects that will acquaint them with world's permanencies, both spiritual and physical.

2.3 PROGRESSIVISM IN EPISTEMOLOGY AND EDUCATION

As against the perrenialists the progressivists believe that change, not permanence, is the essence of reality. Education, therefore, is always in the process of development. Educators must be ready to evolve and modify methods and policies in the light of new knowledge and changes in the environment. The essence of education is a continual reconstruction of experience so that we may understand it in a better and more useful way.

From the above account it is quite evident that knowledge plays a fundamental role in education and that any particular view or theory about the nature and sources of knowledge has its characteristic counterpart in the sphere of education.

CHAPTER

3

KNOWLEDGE, VALUES AND EDUCATION

THE QUEST AFTER VALUES, and the attainment thereof, constitute the very core of human life. There is an innate necessity for man to participate in the process of value-realisation. That is why consciously or unconsciously value-concepts, value-discriminations and value-judgements feature prominently in his life.

The process of value-realisation is basically an educational one. There is an educational dimension indigeneous to axiology and, reciprocally, there is a necessary connection between educational objectives and value-seeking. Education must have some objectives if it is to be effective and of any worth. It tends to refer to a set of values or ideals embodied and expressed in the objectives for which knowledge, skill etc. are imparted. It is quite natural, therefore, to ask 'what is it that education thrives to accomplish ?' A consideration of this problem necessitates a sort of value-thinking, for it is value-decisions alone which can provide valid and adequate objectives

The value-considerations are so widely pervading the sphere of education that all educational decisions involve or presuppose value-decisions. For example, what is to be taught (ends or objectives), how is it to be taught (methods), whom is it to be taught (fitness, motivation and interest of the pupil), how to evaluate, or mark or grade the performance of the pupil etc. are the problems which demand value-considerations.

Moreover in all educational activity value-involvement is inevitable, whether this activity consists of instruction by a professional teacher or of that influence and stimulation which issue forth in the intercourse of human beings. The more the teacher or the educator is aware of the realm of values, so much more he opens the vision, understanding and perspective for the life of the person he guides. In all subjects of study as well as in all problems of life imperceptably valuational questions are involved and whenever the teacher advises, calls attention to, speaks about, or reproves, he is inevitably diverting and moulding the value-sensibility of the pupil. And therefore, the more unripe the pupil, so much the more responsible should be the teacher. A too narrow valuational perception on the part of the teacher is always a serious danger for the youth entrusted to him. The consequence is a premature forcing into a one sided, limited or even biased interpretation of life. It is, therefore, highly necessary that we must educate the educator.

0.1 Noetic Basis of Vaule Considerations

When once we have grasped the fact that the nature of man, and therefore his education, is such as to urge him to participate in the fulness of life, to be receptive of the significant, and to lie open to whatever has meaning and value, then the question arises as to how do we know what is valuable in life and in the world ? What are we to make our own, to understand, to appreciate so as to be man in the full meaning of the word ? What is it for which we still lack the ability so that we must first form our capacity, sharpen and educate it ? The question, in short, is how can we discern the values of humam life and education ? The same problem in a different form confronted Socrates when he posed the problem, can virtue be taught ? The solution arrived at by him is of great relevance to our problem. He maintained that virtue is knowledge and therefore it can be taught. Though values are not knowledge in the ratiocinative form of knowledge, yet a knowing of this sort belongs to them. Though the process of value-realisation is not knowledge, it presupposes knowledge. Knowledge is the presupposition of all value-decisions. This conclusion leads us to consider the noetic-basis of values.

If knowledge is the prior condition of values we must inquire what sort of knowledge is this ? There are two alternative answers given to this question. Some hold that such a knowledge is acquired by practice and can be taught. Conversely, others maintain that it is something inborn in man by nature. These two disjunctive answers lead to two, 'either-or' positions with regard to the knowledge of values. The former alternative leads to relativism whereas the other one culminates is absolutism in values.

Plato (Meno 82b-86e) undertook a cross-examination of a slave for the analysis of the phenomenon of teaching and learning. His cross-examination led him to establish that knowledge is an original possession in man. 'Learning' is only a becoming conscious of the factual contents in him. The teaching by the teacher is only the directing of attention to the matter. The pupil must see it himself, must be convinced by it himself, otherwise there is no real insight. Teaching is merely the midwifery of cognition.

This learning which consists in the apprehension of the

inborn knowledge is called 'anamnesis'. It means to recover of oneself knowledge from within oneself. From this analysis we can conclude that the knowledge of values is through an aprioristic insight. All value-perceptions are necessarily aprioristic. There is another significant implication which must be brought to the fore. Though the reality or existence is inherently saturated with values, it lacks a distinct valuational form. It is, as it were, an unactualised mass of value. Therefore the cognisance of value demands an effort for its fullest realisation. This urge for realisation of value is also apriori. So a distinction can be maintained between two complementary apriori processes viz. valuational discernment and valuational effectiveness.

3.0 Value-Problems in Education

The confusion over values in our society is very much mirrored in education. The multiple problems of teachers, pupils, curriculum etc. are nothing but its reflections. All these problems cannot be resolved without a serious attempt to adjudicate value-conflicts. Some of the value problems that have an impact on the field of education are as follows :

3.1 The first problem concerning values is with regard to their very existence. It has been very much doubted by some thinkers specially in the west as to whether there is anything like a value which is real and existent. Some of them take it to be a mere sentimental vagary or emotive expression having no cognitive worth ; whereas there are others who regard it as an abstraction of human thought. These people very much doubt as to whether values can be taught or realised.

Fortunately, in India there are very few who are genuinely sceptic about the existence of values of life and, therefore, of education. The Indian thinkers from the Vedas downwards, could find an abiding and enduring place for values in the very heart of the ultimate reality. The essentially valuational character of the Reality is quite evident from the Upaniṣadic description of the Reality (Brahman) as Sat, Cit and Ānanda. It is in Ānanda (values) that there is the culmination of all existence (sat) and knowledge (cit). Any acceptance of Sat and Cit devoid of Ānanda (Value) dimension is bound to be deficient. So much is the Reality tending towards values that the Taittirīya Upaniṣad describes Brahman as, 'Raso vai saḥ', or as 'Ānandam brahmaṇo rūpam'. It goes to the extent of saying, "who indeed could live, who breathe, should not this Ānanda be in the sky." The Taittirīya Āraṇyaka is much more emphatic when it declares, "Ānanda is the beginning and the end of the world, the cause as well as the effect, the root as well as the shoot." The whole world would not have been a place worth living if there were no values to be realised in the world.

On the basis of scriptural testimony as well as intuitional realisations, the claim of value upon existence was always upheld in India. It was, however, emphasised that the fullest expression and the highest fruition of value is found in Brahman only which is an index of perfection or fulness 'Yō vai bhumā tatsukham'. This is also the purport of the Ānanda Valli section of the Taittirīya Upaniṣad.

In the human beings, because of their limitations and imperfections the values are only partially reflected. But every individual is at bottom one with Brahman, which means he has the potentialities for growth and development so as to be perfect. The very word 'Brahman' stands for growth and perfection. So the ultimate aim of every individual should be the fullest efflorescence of the value-essence lying hidden or dormant in him. In the Upaniṣads and the Gītā there is a very suggestive description of a tree with roots upward and shoots downward. This suggests that our growth is rooted in, and nourished from, above. It is this Brahmanisation, i.e., perfection by growth which is the real meaning of mokṣa or self-realisation. It should be made clear that this realisation is not regarded as a mere utopian dream because it is firmly believed that every individual being has descended from perfection and has a natural claim to be back at perfection. This is one of the implications of the famous scriptural saying, 'Aum pūrṇamadaḥ pūrṇamidam pūrṇātpūrṇamudacyate pūrṇasya pūrṇamādāya pūrṇamevāvaśiṣyate'.

From the above analysis we can derive a conclusion which is of great importance to the educational context. It is that values are realisable and therefore they ought to be realised. For Brahman values are in existence, but for a human being, who is 'Brahman in the making', they are yet to be realised. They are attainable through endeavour and that is why they are called puruṣārthas. This value-realisation is a spiritual necessity. But it is not possible until and unless all the obstacles in the process of growth and fulness are removed. Here comes the role of education which is recognised to be the only mode of purification.

3.2 There is another problem which is very much discussed these days by our educators and curriculum-framers. That is with regard to the source of values. Who should provide the scheme of values to be incorporated in the curriculum and to be realised through education ? Should we rely upon the politicians or those who are at the height of educational beauracracy, who themselves have no clear knowledge of the nature of values ?

Among the western thinkers we find a great deal of divergence on this problem. Some of them—specially the Christian thinkers—propagated a supernatural origin of values. Some secular thinkers regard values as rooted in nature, whereas others insist that they are founded on human nature—individual or social. But such a theory has resulted in a severe controversy as to whether the values are subjective or objective. In the field of education its corollaries are (*i*) do educational values exist independent of the valuer, or do they exist in a valuing organism ? (*ii*) what is the relation between the interest, motive and happiness of the learner and the subject learnt ?

In India such a situation never arose, because the Indian thinkers were always aware of the pitfalls of the narrow compartmentalisation. They were conscious of the dangers lurking in the subjectivistic position as well as the unpsychological consequences the abstract objectivistic position was fraught with. In accepting the subjectivity of value in education, we would have been at the mercy of every passing whim or vagary of the fickle and vascillating individual mind. And this would tell upon the unity and stability of values. Further every individual being is not so intellectually developed as to conceive what is desirable and what is undesirable. As Lord Krișṇa points out that with regard to its intricacy even wise people get confused in this. On the contrary if we were to uphold the objectivism of values then this would tend to a sort of regimentation and consequently the individual initiative and motivation would be put to peril.

In order to safeguard the unity and stability of the value and at the same time to retain the individual initiative and motivation, the Indian thinkers maintain that the ultimate Reality is the source and abode of all values.

Such a position is of great educational importance and relieves us from the unrealistic subjective-objective hairsplitting. Since the values are rooted in the ultimate Reality and since every individual being partakes that nature, the values are at once both subjective and objective. The order of values is closely akin to, or rather dependent on, the order of being. Therefore, no account of valuational theory would be true unless it is not based on the universal human nature, which is a reflection of a wider nature of the ultimate Reality. Further, though the values originate in the ultimate Reality, subtle seers or the wise people, alone can cognise them and it is their function to formulate the aims and objectives of life and education.

3.3 Though the values possess a sort of unity and uniformity, they are not rigidly uniform. They manifest certain differences and therefore admit of a classification. There can be different classifications of values on different bases. The basic classification that can be put forth is between absolute or intrinsic values and relative or instrumental values. Accordingly, all the values of life, and therefore of education, can be brought under two heads, viz., preyas and śreyas, as was done by the ancient Indian thinkers. The preyas pertains to material welfare and śreyas pertains to spiritual realisation.

Though these two types of values refer to two different orders of being, there is no incompatibility between the two. There is no schism in the two orders of being, and hence no bifurcation between matter and spirit. Therefore they do not admit of any exclusiveness of 'either-or' position. Preyas provides the material basis and śreyas constitutes the spiritual summit of the same process of Brahmanisation or perfection. That is why in the Taittirīya Upaniṣad the preceptor in his final instruction exhorts the pupil as 'kuśalānna pramaditavyam, bhūtyai na pramaditavyam.' Here bhūti stands for preyas and kuśala stands for śreyas.

Since matter provides the arena for the self-realisation of the spirit, the preyas has the natural claim to be first catered to.

But one should not remain entangled with preyas for ever. After the necessary gratification of the preyas he should make a passage towards śreyas. However, it should be remembered that such a passage must be gradual and not sudden. The example of Bhartṛhari is there to remind us of the consequences of the sudden passage. Another thing that is to be remembered is that all the demands of matter do not constitute preyas and hence are not to be gratified. Only those demands are to be regarded as preyas which are not incompatible with śreyas which is the superior value.

The preyas, thus, is the proximate value and śreyas is the absolute and ultimate value. So far as the śreyas is concerned it is above the interest, motive or happiness of the seeker. It does not go against the true interests of the seeker. But the preyas or the proximate values, being based on the empirical nature of the individual, differ from one individual to another individual, because of their differences in guṇās and consequently in svabhāvās. That is why the ancient thinkers formulated the four-fold classification of the society. In order that there may be a conscious well-organised and balanced pursuit of both the preyas and the śreyas they established the āśrama vyavasthā. The word āśrama is suggestive of the points of beginning and stoppage. First of all the individual must be made aware of his preyas and śreyas. Then he should be taught first to realise preyas upto a certain extent of his life and then to turn towards the realisation of śreyas. He should also be taught that he himself is a whole but he belongs to a still larger whole. Therefore there should not be any occasion of the collision of his preyas with the preyas of the society. That is why through various similies like the 'puruṣayajña' in the Ṛgveda or the 'Virāta puruṣa' in the Gītā, he is reminded of the basic unity of the mankind. Right from the very beginning of his pupil-hood he is initiated into community life, as is clear from the following prayer, 'Auṃ sahanāvavatu saha nau bhunaktu saha vīryam karavāvahai. Tejasvināvadhītamastu, Mā vidviṣāvahai' etc.

2.4 In the foregoing account we have seen that the individual is in the process of growth or perfection, which we have termed as Brahmanisation. This Brahmanisation consists in a balanced realisation of preyas and śreyas. The possibilities or potentialities for perfection are there in him and what is needed is their evolution or fructification through purifications. This fact is beautifully illustrated in the Chhāndogya Upaniṣad with the example of a small seed which contains within itself the possibilities of turning out into a big tree.

We have fixed up self-realisation as the goal of life and of education. But how to achieve it ? Or, what are the different steps in the process of its realisation ? For this, we should explicate the meaning of the word 'self'. The Upaniṣadic thinkers use the word 'self', in a very wide sense. It encompasses the entire human nature and extends to the entire cosmos. They firmly believe in the fundamental unity of the microcosm and the macrocosm. They analyse the human nature into five aspects, one over-laping the other in succession. They name them as sheaths. They are as follows, annamaya, prāṇamaya, manomaya, vijñānamaya and ānandamaya. The same aspects are there in Brahman and in the outer cosmos as well. That is why the Upaniṣads declare, 'annam vai brahma', prāṇo vai brahma' etc. Though these aspects are present in Brahman in their fullest, for Brahman is fulness, they are not so in the individual, and are to be developed. An all-round development of man means fullest development of all these aspects in a proper proportion. These aspects do not exist in a juxtapository order but in a heirarchical order. Therefore, the process of realisation should start from that which is the lowest and should culminate in that which is the highest. Since bodily aspect comes first, it should be first developed. But one should not feel contented with the development of the body only. After its necessary development it has got to be transcended to the higher one and so on. It should be made clear that in this transcendence from lower to higher, the lower is not negated or annihilated by the higher but is absorbed by it. Each higher principle is more inclusive and comprehensive than the lower, and in the realisation of the higher the lower *ipso facto* gets realised. The lower takes its proportionate place in a pattern of living in which the higher gives the general direction of emphasis. Thus the ānandamaya kośa which is the highest kośa is the most comprehensive and includes all within its fold. That alone is the real self and all others are only partial appearances of the self. When we speak of self-realisation we mean the realisation of this total self.

Of these five kośas the first two pertain to the level of gross existences, and are associated with the gross body and the waking state. They may be referred to as Sat. The next two belong to the level of subtle existence or knowledge and are associated with subtle and causal body, and with dream state and deep sleep state. They may be referred to as Cit. The last one, i.e., ānandamaya kośa is the real self which is residing in all the bodies and which is realised in the transcendental state. This may be referred to as Ānanda. A proper and full development of all the aspects of sat, cit and ānanda is the over-all goal of a human being. There is another concept which also suggests to the same. The realisation of the over-all self is viewed as the foremost duty and obligation. We have sparked off from Brahman and owe a debt to him. This debt has three aspects, viz., to Pitṛ, to Guru and to Deva. The pitṛ ṛṇa obliges us to develop the first two kośas, the guru ṛṇa demands the perfection of the next two kosas and the deva ṛṇa urges for the realisation of the last kośa.

The above account may be regarded as a fair reconstruction of the Upaniṣadic order of being and value. This account has a great educational significance for us to-day. The doctrine of the pañca kośas tells us that the value of education lies in training and exercising the five kośas in such a way as to make them a fit instrument for a good life which consists in fulness and perfection. It further tells us that in the process of value-realisation, which is nothing but self-realisation, proper balance should be maintained to avoid the dangers of lop-sided development. The correlation between preyas and śreyas reminds us that there is no antagonism between body and spirit, that body is the 'vale of soul-making,' and that there is nothing unnatural in spiritual attainments being realised in a natural order. These two accounts along with the Upaniṣadic classification of knowledge as aparā and parā inculcate on us that our curriculum must be so framed as to do justice to all the orders, our being and value. The Īśopaniṣad strongly advocates the complementary nature of the lower knowledge of the physical and social sciences and the higher knowledge of the spirit. The knowledge of physical sciences and technology, which deals with annamaya and prāṇamaya aspects is quite basic and must be imparted. But that is not enough. For providing a balanced and perfect education the role of social sciences, philosophy etc. which deal with manomaya and vijñānamaya aspects and of the humanities which deal with the ānandamaya aspect, cannot be denied or under-estimated. Such a balancing approach towards curriculum alone can give a proper representation to the different facets or dimensions of human personality.

CHAPTER

4

VALIDATION OF KNOWLEDGE AND EDUCATION

0.1 IT HAS BEEN THE SOLE PREROGATIVE of the human being not only to formulate knowledge out of his varied experiences but also to be benefitted by one's own knowledge as well as by the knowledge acquired by others and transferred to us. Though man is thus bestowed with the faculties of formulating knowledge and of transferring it to and receiving it from others, this process is not always smooth. Whatever data are given by the senses or whatever information is passed on by others as knowledge are not always the true representations of the facts and hence the genuine knowledge. So the possibility of error in human cognition cannot be ruled out. Sometimes the erroneous is brighter than the true and even blurs our vision of truth. The possibility of error not only calls upon us to be constantly vigilant, but also compels us to spell out precisely the criterion to discriminate the true from the erroneous.

Different attempts have been made by the epistemological thinkers to determine such a criterion but a failure to recognise the fact that all experiences cannot be measured with one and the same yardstick, has led to a diversity of positions and different types of criterion are put forth as the exclusive instrument of measurement where as in fact, all combined together alone co nstitutes a unified criterion.

0.2 Here we shall see in brief what different epistemological schools have to say on the problem of validity of knowledge, and how their viewpoints have affected educational theory and practice. Since one of the prime concerns of education is to discover and transmit knowledge it is very necessary to see that all that goes under the lable of knowledge is genuinely valid knowledge. There is a clear distinction between opinion, belief and knowledge, and the task of education should be to equip the pupil with a clear understanding of the differences between these three.

The main issue then is, what must be the criterion for judging whether a piece of information is genuine knowledge as distinguished from opinion, belief or false knowledge. The western epistemologists have propounded three main different theories to solve this issue which are named respectively as correspondence theory of truth, coherence theory of truth and pragmatic theory of truth. We shall give a brief account of these theories vis-a-vis education.

4.1.0 The correspondance theory which is a sophisticated version of common sense view states that if any piece of information squares with reality then it is true. Such a view is based on that realistic metaphysics according to which the external reality or world is independent of human knower, and the truth lies in the external relation of correspondance between our ideas or impressions and the facts which the ideas or impressions represent.

4.1.1 The educational implications of such a theory are as follows: Learning would be said to be correct if the learner's impressions tally with the external reality. Truth is regarded as something external, objective and pre-existent to the search for it. It is immutable and not changing. The learner merely unveils the truth which is ever-existent. He does not create it. His awareness or knowledge of truth does not, in any way, affect the reality since the reality is independent of knowledge.

4.1.2 The correspondance theory of truth though apparently seems to be convincing, is vitiated with a serious difficulty. Truth or otherwise of knowledge is based on the correspondence between knowledge and reality. But the point is, how can we be sure that our ideas and impressions really correspond to reality? How can we say that our knowledge is true and hence is related to reality unless there is another true knowledge to guarantee the truth or relatedness of our present knowledge. But that another true knowledge will, in turn, presuppose still another true knowledge and so on *ad infinitum*. To avoid this if it is said that the knowledge of truth (certifying knowledge) that it is truth (certified knowledge) are one and the same, then every piece of knowledge will claim the certificate of truth and there will no longer be any distinction between truth and falsity. Further, one's own impressions of the same fact at different occasions or of different persons' impressions of the same fact at one and the same occasion seldom correspond. How can we then, determine which impression is closer to truth?

4.2.0 Those who interpose the above questions believe that the criterion of truth must be something more than mere external correspondance to reality. We can never know the exact correspondance with the naked reality but at the most we can know only the consistency between our ideas or impressions about reality. This is the consistency theory of truth. According to the advocates of this theory, who are mostly idealists and agnostics, all that we know of the reality are mere its copies which take much of their character from the apriori nature of human mind. The so-called acquisition of knowledge is as much a building forth from within as it is a taking in from without. In operating on its sense data, mind checks them for internal consistency. The more consistent they are the more nearly they approximate the universal law and order which is the characteristic of the world wherein all knowledge subsist as an inter-related whole.

4.2.1 The advocates of this theory proclaim that such a view guarantees both the reliability as well as the objectivity of knowledge. The knowledge will be reliable if the successive impressions of the same knower tend to be consistent with each other, and objective if they are consistent with the impressions of other knowers operating under the same conditions.

4.2.2 The educational implications of this theory are as follows: Since the knower is intimately related to the known, he should not merely familiarise himself with a mass of information but should try to learn about it by himself. He should also try to unify his present knowledge with the past one and instead of absorbing selected piece of knowledge he should try to explore the reality as a whole.

4.2.3 The consistency or coherence theory of truth seems to be an improvement upon the correspondence theory but it also harbours the same fallacy with which the correspondence theory is vitiated. Here also the problem is, by what criterion does it decide the truth of the criterion of truth? Obviously it cannot be the criterion of consistency for that would amount to begging the question.

4.3.0 Dissatisfied with the practical futility and barrenness of the above two positions, some thinkers, known as pragmatists or instrumentalists or experimentalists, propose to test the truth of ideas on the basis of their practical consequences. For them truth is what works. It does not exist, it happens. It is never perfect, eternal, immutable but it is in the process of making.

4.3.1 Under the dynamic leadership of Dewey this school of thought has immensely affected the educational theory and practice. According to it ideas by themselves are neither true nor false. They only become so when employed to solve a problem or prosecute a project related to educational practice. For example, if they clear up the confusion and restore the continuity of instruction then they are true. The pragmatic test of truth as workability is most familiar to educators in the project or problem method of teaching.

4.3.2 But the pragmatic criterion of truth is also not free from flaws. It confuses truth with value and subjects it to expediency. Though Dewey has been careful to avoid this confusion, he could do so only by ousting some basic pragmatic ideas and by bringing in some elements of consistency theory. That a theory or hypothesis works when it is corroborated by its consequences suggests that possibly Dewey's theory of truth is, in a sense, a further development of the consistency theory. For him consistency is, not just the relation that holds between ideas, but also the relation which holds between ideas and their consequences.

4.4.0 All these different theories of the criterion of truth seem to be mutually conflicting. But it is so because they are looked at in abstraction. If we take them in their concrete frame of reference we will find them mutually dependent and complementary. For example, the criterion of correspondance is true because it is self-consistent and could be worked out. The criterion of consistency is true because it corresponds with the real structure of knowledge, and hence, it also works. The criterion of work ability is also true because it is self-consistent and shows how correspondence is a matter of fact. Similarly, that knowledge which is internally harmonious or consistent is likely to be true, but its likelihood increases if in addition. to the internal harmony that knowledge is further believed to be in harmony with the external reality. The realisation of this mutual harmony of knowledge and reality is made possible by the further harmony of knowledge with practice. So the ultimate criterion of truth is neither mere correspondence nor mere consistency or mere workability but all the three taken together constitute one harmonious criterion. So in the field of education as well we should be conscious of this fact and test the truth of the instructional material on the basis of the particular frame of reference.

CHAPTER

5

KNOWLEDGE AND CURRICULUM-FRAMING

0.1 ALL EDUCATIONAL THINKERS CONCUR in regarding knowledge as the indispensable organ of education. This is specially so with respect to the curriculum. Knowledge influences not only the organisation of curriculum but also its teaching. Curriculum is the avenue through which the pupil approaches the stock of knowledge. In the present chapter, therefore, an attempt will be made to see how a philosophical analysis of the phenomenon of knowledge can provide a framework for the curriculum planning. Here we shall not enter into the details about exactly what should be taught in any given academic situation, for this would mean transgressing into the field of the curriculum-planner.

5.1.0 The basic question pertaining to knowledge vis-a-vis curriculum is with regard to the type of knowledge that has to be imparted to the pupil through the curriculum. In other words, the problem is, how shall we determine the content of the curriculum? There is another problem in the field of curriculum-framing which need to be tackled epistemologically. The problem arises because knowledge is diverse and infinite and therefore everything cannot be learnt at once. This necessitates ordering of the content of instruction. Such an ordering presupposes an insight into the complexities and intraconnections of the diverse forms and facets of knowledge. The problem of the explosion of knowledge also requires a critical analysis of the existing stock of knowledge as well as the new in-coming knowledge so that we may not only maintain proportion and perspective in curriculum-framing but also can avoid the superficial and get at the essential.

Knowledge already attained constitutes the subject matter of the curriculum. Here the problem is whether we should regard knowledge as antedated to the experiences of the learner or as acquired with the process of learning by the learner. Most of the schools, with the exception of the pragmatists believe in the former alternative. For them knowledge is the funded capital of social experience which is embodied in the books. The only business of the teacher and the pupil is to unlock this storehouse of knowledge. Such an attitude leads to a kind of theoretical education. The reason for organising the curriculum in this fashion is to release the student from the demands of the immediate situation. However, this theoretical education should not be conceived as impractical or to be taught apart from example. Otherwise this would severe intelligence from action and volition, knowledge from every day concerns of life. This would also lead to the evils of memorising facts and information.

The pragmatist's view regarding knowledge vis-a-vis curriculum, on the other hand, is that in a changing world it would be inadvisable to apply the past verified knowledge resulting from the previous problematic inquiry to the next problem for inquiry. We can, at the most, regard it as the data for solving subsequent problems, but never as solutions. So there should be no rigidly fixed curriculum, but it should be evolved as the learning proceeds.

There is another problem with regard to the arrangement of the various types of knowledge in the curriculum. Those who believe that knowledge is dependent upon reliability, maintain that there are several grades of knowledge. These grades are measured on the basis of the degree of abstraction they achieve. Accordingly a hierarchy is established in which natural sciences constitute the first stage, mathematics the middle stage and metaphysics the final stage.

5.2.0 To all these problems different schools of epistemology will not give identical solutions. That is because their basic assumptions and presuppositions are so diverse as to lead them to dis-similar positions and conclusions. However one thing should again be noted that these diverse positions and conclusions are reached from different standpoints and instead of contradicting one another they rather mutually compliment and supplement.

5.2.1 The school of Naturalism, being anti-authoritarian in its approach to knowledge, emphasises the present experience, activities and interests of the pupil. It insists that the child should have his own proper experience unhampered and unhindered by adult interference and direction. There are no set goals of knowledge and hence of education. The only goal is that of fostering the growth of a free, active, happy and well-adjusted human being.

Pragmatism, on the other hand, takes the future utility also into consideration. The curriculum must include the knowledge and skills that the child requires, not only for his present life as a child but also for his future life as an adult. That is why pragmatism emphasises vocational education. It stresses the child rather than the subject or the teacher. So the content of the curriculum must be concerned with the realities of human life.

Idealism, however, approaches the problem of curriculum from the domain of idea rather than from the view point of the child and his present or future activities. It concentrates on the rounded whole of human knowledge and experience.

5.2.2 Different thinkers and schools of thought have suggested different bases for curriculum organisation. On the basis of the familiar psychological analysis of experience into conation, cognition and affection it has been maintained that the curriculum must comprise (a) What man does and strives to do. This would include all crafts and technology. (b) What man knows, i.e., his major modes of thinking. This would consist of all sciences, philosophy and literature. (c) What man feels. This envelopes all the fine arts like poetry and music. This classification also has the basis of tripartite division of human being into hand, head and heart.

Whitehead has propounded the idea that learning has a natural three-fold rhythm whose successive phases are 'romance', 'precision' and 'generalisation'. Nunn also has given the same account in different words when he developed the three-fold periodicity of wonder, ulility and system as the natural stages in the learning process. Such an analysis can also provide a basis for curriculum organisation.

But the best way to organise curriculum is to base it on the analysis of the constituents of human being. In the Upaniṣads we find one of the best accounts of such an analysis. The Upaniṣads conceive of the human being as consisting of five elements which envelope one another in succession. That is why they are named as sheaths or coverings (kosa). The first and outermost sheath is gross physical sheath named as annamayakośa. The second one is that of vital breaths i.e. physiological. This is named as prāṇamayakośa. The third one is mental which consists of feelings and imagination. This is called manomaya kośa. The fourth one is the sheath consisting of intellect and rational pursuits. This is named as vijñānamayakośa. The last one is the self which consists of pure bliss and which is named as ānandamaya kośa.

A balanced organisation of the curriculum demands that the needs of all these aspects of human being must be catered to. This means physical sciences and technology dealing with the first two aspects, social sciences and humanities dealing with the next two and religion and value-pursuits dealing with the last one must all be included in the curriculum. The main object of education is to impart knowledge, knowledge which is conducive to the fullest development of the individual. Therefore no education can be regarded as perfect or complete which neglects or overlooks any of these five aspects of human being.

Since man is the centre of education it must be a man-making education. If that is so then the role of all the disciplines which may lead or contribute to this end must be properly recognised. Otherwise education would be lopsided. The present day tendency is swinging too much in the direction of science and technology. Since these disciplines deal with the physical aspect of the human being, they must come first but one must not regard them as the only pursuits of knowledge. They are the instrumental ends for the acquisition of some higher ends and therefore in their pursuits the higher ends must not be lost sight of.

There has been a tendency to uphold a false dichotomy between science and technology on the one hand and humanities and social sciences on the other on the ground that the former deal with the values of the 'matter' whereas the latter with the values of the 'spirit'. But it is fallacious to make such a sharp distinction between the two. The values of the matter and of the spirit are not so distinct as to admit of separate pursuits. As the ancient Indian thinkers had emphasised, the preyas and the śreyas are complementary goals, the former providing a base to the latter. No pursuits of the materialistic values can be regarded as preyas unless it culminates in the welfare of the spirit as well. Similarly no śreyas can be worth its name, unless it has preyas as its base. To regard preyas and śreyas as antagonistic is to bred a false antithesis between matter and spirit, but in fact neither matter is the prisonhouse for spirit nor is spirit the annihilator of matter. Matter rather is the 'vale of spirit-making' and spirit is the blossomed flower of the matter. Whitehead also has repudiated the false dichotomy between science and technology on the one hand and humanities and social sciences on the other. As he puts it, there can be no adequate technical education which is not liberal and no liberal education which is not technical.

Education is a preparation for life. But life is not mere livelihood. Similarly life is not mere catering to the needs of either matter or spirit. There is no exclusive 'either-or' between general education and a specialist education. No man is merely a professional man, whether an engineer or a doctor or a scientist or a technician. He is above all a man, a social man. Hence the fulness of education must include besides the skills and techniques of professional training, the development of all the five faculties described in the Upaniṣads. From the above it follows that the true and adequate system of education must aim at and provide for the education of the whole man. Though the fullest realisation of this may not be possible, this must not deter or deflect us from aiming at it. How far we may succeed in achieving it is a matter for sober realistic and unsanguine reflection. But let us initially not overlook the final aim of education which is to produce men and women and not tools, to make human beings and not machines.

If this ultimate ideal is once understood and accepted there should arise, in principle at least, no conflict between special and general education, between professional and liberal education, between sciences and humanities. The problem then would be only of adjustment and co-ordination among different disciplines. In order to solve this problem we should keep in mind the views advocated by Whitehead. He maintains that there are three main methods which are required in a national system of education, namely, the scientific curriculum, the literary curriculum and the technical curriculum. But each of these curricula should include the other two. However there should be a distinction between primary elements and secondary elements in the curricula, and the dominant emphasis must be laid on the primary one. Care must be taken that the dominant emphasis whether literary, scientific or technical should be such that it should not lose the element of co-ordination and should infuse into each way of education something of the other two. Such a thing alone can ensure a balanced curriculum. But in order to do so we should not only have the sense of priorities but also of the dominant emphasis. Such an approach to education would solve the problem of explosion of knowledge and would provide the basis for the elimination of the non-essential and retention of the essential.

5.3.0 The structure of curriculum is dependent upon the structure of disciplines. But what is structure of disciplines? It means three things : three distinct but related sets of problems. The first problem is that of identifying the disciplines that constitute the contemporary knowledge. This would provide the subject matter of education. Here we have to establish the relations between various disciplines so that they may be joined together for purposes of instruction. This will also help us in keeping apart those disciplines which cannot be so joined. Further this will enable us to determine the sequence of instruction, i.e., it will tell us what must come before what, or what is most desirably placed first, or second, or third.

The second problem is with regard to the substantive structure of the disciplines. That is to say it is concerned with the structure of the concepts and with the understanding of the powers and limits of the enquiries that take place under their guidance. Every enquiry has its origin in a conceptual structure. It is through this that we are able to formulate a telling question. Through the telling question alone we know what data to seek and what experiments to perform to get those data. Once the data are in hand, the same conceptual structure tells us how to interpret them, what to make of them by way of knowledge. Finally, the knowledge itself is formulated in terms provided by the same conception. In the sphere of education this problem has great significance. For to know what structures underlie a given body of knowledge is to know what problems we shall face in imparting this knowledge. This would enable us to determine which sort of knowledge should be imparted at what stage of the mental development of the child so that the knowledge may be imparted without any difficulty. The third problem of the structure of disciplines is that of their syntactical structure. This problem arises because since different disciplines use different conceptual frames, there are likely to be major differences between one discipline and another. There is, then, the problem of determining for each discipline what it does by way of discovery and proof, what criteria it uses for measuring the quality of its data, how strictly it can apply canons of evidence, and in general, of determining the process by which the discipline moves from its raw data through a longer or shorter method of interpretation to its conclusion.

5.3.1 The world of knowledge has today become radically plural. It is a world of many different knowledges, pursued in varied ways to diverse ends. These many inquiries are usually carried on with little thought for their relation to each other. Each researcher has his own goals, his own methods, his own language of talking about what he is doing and what he has discovered. Though this pluralism in knowledge is not an unwelcome feature, it poses a problem for those who are concerned with the organisation of the entire curriculum. For the curriculum builder is concerned not only with the structures of the individual disciplines, but also with the structure of the instructional programme within which the fields of knowledge find their place. This leads us to the problem of organisation of the disciplines.

The problem of organisation is a problem of classification primarily. Since the disciplines are quite complex, we are faced with a wide choice of bases of classification. Four bases of classification of disciplines are usually put forth: (*i*) their subject matter (*ii*) their practitioners i e., what competences and habits are required to carry on their work (*iii*) their methods (syntax) and modes of enquiry (*iv*) their ends.

There is another factor which matters much in the organisation of disciplines. It is that of relationships among the various disciplines. For just as relationships among ideas are at the heart of the concept of structure as applied to individual disciplines, so relationships among the disciplines are at the heart of the notion of structure as applied to the curriculum as a whole.

There are many ways in which one can conceive of these inter-connections. Of these three types deserve special mention. They are as follows:

(*i*) Relationships among cognate or allied disciplines that deal with similar problems or phenomena. For example, the traditional broad groupings of organised disciplines are the natural sciences, the social sciences, mathematics and humanities.

(*ii*) Relationships among broad areas of knowledge like sciences, mathematics and technology on the one hand and social sciences and humanities on the other. Another such grouping can be on the basis of modes of thought, viz., the analytic, the empirical, the aesthetic and the moral.

(*iii*) Relationships of knowledge to human affairs. The goal of education is not merely to impart knowledge but also to prepare students for intelligent action. This requires a new curriculum centred on broad social issues and drawing upon the academic disciplines as they become relevant to the problems under study.

The present day curricula often focus their attention on the organisation or inter-relations of the various disciplines. Such an approach is very much profitable and therefore there must be much more emphasis on interdisciplinary approaches and collaboration among the disciplines. So there is a need for a broader context for curriculum planning. All the disciplines should be called upon to join in this new venture in which the integrity of all the disciplines will be safeguarded, at the same time a substantial measure of coherence and relatedness will be achieved.

CHAPTER

6

KNOWLEDGE AND TEACHING-LEARNING STRATEGY

0.1 ULTIMATELY, THE FOCAL POINT of all educational phenomena centres round the teaching and learning strategy. The character and outcome of this phenomenon depend on the curriculum and the methods that are employed and the latter, in turn, are dependent upon the way in which they stand in relation to knowledge. Thus though remotely yet fundamentally the entire working of educative process is based on epistemology.

There is another point that should be noted in this connection. The basic thing in all educational activities is the aims. These educational aims not only indicate the values to be sought but they should also involve a personal commitment thereto. This brings in the element of interest. As per the ancient doctrine of apperception, one cannot hope to get interest on the part of the pupil unless the latter already has an interest. Interest depends on knowledge and knowledge is outgrowth of prior instruction. The interesting instructor is therefore the one who can make new things seem old.

6.1.0 Logical Order of the Instructional Material

In order that the teaching-learning process may be smooth and interesting, it is necessary to keep up the logical order of the instructional material. Not only the human mind has a longing for order but it is also an invincible quality of the world. It has been wrongly believed that mind is a logical and that logical order is detrimental to interest and motivation. In fact the logical order is conducive to the development of interest. Moreover, logical order can be based on the psychological order and thus there can be many logical orders depending on the present point of pupil's knowledge and interests. The logical order is from the simple to the complex but 'simple' and 'complex' are relative notions depending upon the mental development of learner. That which is simple for one may be complex for another. Thus both the logical and the psychological orders go hand in hand and it is false to regard them as antagonistic. Both are necessary for any rounded approach to the educative process.

It is quite clear from the above considerations that it is not only desirable but also necessary to organise instructional material in a logical fashion. The more it is logically interrelated the more sensitive it would be to invoke interest in the pupils. Here it should also be remembered that the logic of teaching is not the same as the logic of learning because the teacher represents in achievement and maturity what the pupil only potentially has in his immaturity.

When the content of instruction is organised logically, it is arranged according to a hierarchy of principles and concepts that are said to be present in the branches of knowledge themselves. Each branch has its own hierarchy of knowledge and all these branches are said to form a hierarchy together.

Knowledge is organised in a number of disciplines and each discipline is both a kind of knowledge and a kind of knowing. It is both a system of ideas or theories and a means of acquiring them. Thus it also involves a methodology, a way of inquiry. As knowledge evolves new fields open up for investigation and newer methods of inquiry are found out. In this process new disciplines are established and some old ones are also sometimes abandoned. Some disciplines seek knowledge for its own sake whereas others are concerned with applying knowledge to practical ends. But all applied disciplines rest on theoretical ones. Hence in the curriculum knowledge should be organised as it is organised in the theoretical disciplines.

So far as the actual organisation of the various disciplines, as a whole, is concerned recently a number of classifications have been proposed. Two works in this connection are worth mentioning. They are (1) '*Education and the Structure of Knowledge*' edited by Stanley Elam (2) *Realms of Meaning: A Philosophy of the Curriculum for General Education* by Philip H. Phenix.

6.2.0 Logical Operations in Teaching and Learning

Since the aim of all education is to impart knowledge effectively, the success of the teaching-learning strategy lies in properly knocking at the door of knowledge. The teaching-learning process involves expounding and mastering an item of knowledge. In expounding a piece of knowledge the teacher presents before the pupils a set of conclusions together with the grounds or evidences that support it. He presents arguments, facts, proofs etc., defines concepts, explains them, draws conclusions and generalises. And reciprocally the pupils also in mastering this piece of knowledge ascertain that the grounds or evidences do, in fact, support the conclusions. Thus both these processes invariably involve some logical operations.

6.2.1 Present-day Ignorance of Logical Operations

(*i*) In teachers—The more the teaching-learning process has to be effective, the more should it have a logical basis. The quality of this process could surely be improved if the teachers and pupils are made aware of the logical operations that they perform or could perform when expounding and mastering a piece of knowledge. These days because of the ignorance of the logical operations involved in a genuine teaching-learning method, it is far less intellectually oriented than it ought to be. Our teachers fail to challenge and stimulate the minds of the pupils because not only they are ignorant of these logical operations but also they do not know the logical techniques of argument, exposition, debate etc. which have to be engineered to stimulate the intellectual abilities of the pupils. That is why even when an intelligent student makes a point, however, imperfect in logicality, the teacher often can not pursue it to its logical completion because he is unable to grasp the logical operation that the student is unconsciously carrying out.

(*ii*) In students—The pupil too is hindered in his intellectual development by not being aware of the logical operations that he performs, or should perform, in mastering a particular content of instruction and in initiating and carrying on class-room discussion. He is further handicapped by his lack of training in the technique of appraising the arguments and contentions of others. Hence, although he commits to memory a good range of information and to some extent learns to solve problems in particular areas which he has studied, he rarely transfers what he learns in one discipline to other disciplines which he has to learn subsequently.

Hence, the thinking he does in History, for example, is of little benefit to the thinking he is required to do in geography or political science. This is so because he, and unfortunately his teacher also, does not understand that roughly the same techniques of thinking and standards of assessing thoughts, are involved in all realms of knowledge. This is why his different studies do not contribute to one another as they should.

6.2.2 Need for Initiation into Logic

Since certain logical operations are necessarily involved in a clear, consistent and systematic thinking and since certain standards are employed in appraising the products of such a thinking whatever the subject matter, this provides a sufficient rationale and justification for instituting special courses for teachers in the knowledge and performance of logical operations. The teachers, in their training courses, should be made aware of the need to master the various logical operations that are involved in the process of teaching and learning. It is no doubt important for the teacher to understand the psychology of the pupil but it is in no way less important for him to know the logicality of thinking upon which the learning process mostly depends.

6.2.3 Pattern for Framing up such a Course in Logic

There are certain logical operations and standards of evaluation which are, roughly speaking, universally applicable. They should be taught in the various subjects the pupil studies. Or, they can be taught as a separate subject in their own right. Apart from these broad and general operations and standards that cut across different areas of knowledge, there are specific operations and standards that are characteristics of particular branches of knowledge. The teacher or educator should devise ways of teaching them as a part of the subject matter of these branches of knowledge.

The syllabus which will provide a background course in such a methodology must envelop the following considerations within its fold.

(*i*) The growth of logical powers in a child is always gradual and therefore the teacher must be made to know what logical operations the pupil can perform at each stage in his development and with what sophistication. For example, classifying, ordering in serial relations and numbering are the most fundamental logical operations. Upon these are based the more complex operations like deduction and induction. So an attempt must be made to find out as to how many possible logical operations are there involved in teaching and learning process. Some of these can be enumerated as follows: (1) defining (2) describing (3) designating (identifying) (4) stating (5) reporting (6) substituting (7) evaluating (8) opining (9) classifying (10) comparing (11) contrasting (12) inferring (13) explaining. After finding out the possible logical operations as exhaustively as we can, an attempt must be made to divide and subdivide each of these operations so that their nature and function may be thoroughly studied. For example, explaining can be further divided into (1) mechanical (2) causal (3) sequential (4) procedural (5) teleological (6) normative etc. Such a study can be named *calculus of logical operations.*

(*ii*) The teaching-learning process in a class room always centres round a particular topic which can be called episode. Whatever be the discipline, its classroom instruction must be so specific and pertinent that it must be crystallised into one or more distinct episodes. Each episode is initiated with a question which can be called *move* or *entry*. For every entry there is an ideal logical pattern determined by the logical operations required by the entry. For example, an episode of explaining kind must have three elements. Something that is explained, a principle of explanation, and statement connecting the principle and instance. For example, while teaching economics, a teacher may initiate an episode on devaluation by an entry or move in the form of a question, 'why does any country devalue its currency?' And if an intelligent student in the class, who is also well informed, replies, 'so that its export would sell for less', then the teacher should catch up the link and supply the missing principle that "if the prices of export go down, the volumes of export tends to go up." He may further explain that this would clear the dumping of goods and thus help to rotate the money, since it will fetch foreign markets for sale at low price. The pattern of this episode can be schematised thus:

Thing to be explained ↓ Devaluation of Currency

Connecting statement ↓ Export would sell for less

Explanatory Principle ↓ If prices of exports go down, the volume of export goes up.

It should be made clear here that all episodes do not have one uniform pattern. The pattern would differ in accordance with the nature and requirements of the episode. For example, in the case of an evaluating episode there would be four elements, viz., (1) something to be appraised (2) an appraisal (3) criterion of appraisal and (4) grounds regarding the adequacy of the criterion. Thus we shall have to undertake a study of the various possible types of episodes and by analysing their nature and requirements we shall have to find out the elements of logical operation involved in each of them. Such a study can be named *Calculus of episodic structure*.

(*iii*) The problem of assessment is also quite basic to learning process. One of the major tasks of education is to acquaint the pupil with the true criterion of knowledge. No education can be perfect and complete if it merely concerns itself with bare acquisition of knowledge without inculcating the ability to test its validity. The optimum development of personality, which has been the recognised aim of education, requires the cultivation of a reasonably adequate pattern of judgement, and this can be provided only by imparting the definite criterion of meaning and truth. This is what is called the education for critical faculty. Here the problem is, how should the pupil know that the arguments; proofs, conclusions and generalisations of the teacher or of his own are valid (if deductive) or reliable (if inductive)?' This would lead us to formulate all basic categories of judgement with the help of which the pupil will acquire an adequate sense of discernment. Such a study can be named *calculus of logical discernment*.

6.2.4 Efficacy of this Technique for Educational Practice

It may be contended that theoretically the present logical structure of a class room discourse is quite compact and convincing but how far would it be useful in actual educational practice? The answer is, such a logical structure will provide to the teacher an appropriate technique for introducing an episode so that he will be able to communicate the subject matter more effectively. Not only this will enable the teacher to transmit knowledge in a logical fashion, but this will also guide the student so that he will handle this knowledge in a logical manner himself. This will enable him to grasp at once the logical operation that is required of him. By bringing out the logical implications of a topic the teacher will make the treatment of it more searching and more complete. And consequently, the student's grasp will be at once more thorough, more comprehensive and more enduring. This is the creative aspect of the utility of this technique. The critical utility of this technique lies in the fact that this will provide a standard for assessing the logicality of instruction in any class room episode. This will tell (a) how far the teacher is succeeding in actualising the logical structure (b) what steps he should take in guiding the discussion in order to realise this structure still further. The teacher will now be in a better position to improve the students' ability to think logically *per se* because he will know what the operations of logical thinking are, and how the students can be led to perform these operations more effectively. He will also be able to identify mistakes in reasoning, defining, explaining and other logical operations and to classify these errors to the student who commits them.

6.2.5 Concluding Remarks

The present chapter provides only a tentative theoretical basis for experimental inquiry regarding an ideal logical structure of a class-room teaching-learning process. It is based on the assumptions that some logical operations and standards are invariably involved in all kinds of teaching-learning processes and that there can be and should be a logical structure for every class room instruction. However, these assumptions and the logical structure erected here on them are open for review and revision. It is intended that this may be reviewed keeping the following questions in view:

1. To what extent learning to think logically depends on (a) the degree to which the teacher himself carries out each logical operation completely, (b) the degree to which the student is required to confirm to the ideal logical structure of each initiated episode (c) the student's own knowledge of the logical structure of the episode?

2. How much better does the student understand the

content of instruction if he is taught these logical operations as tools in their own right?

3. If more precision is desired in the logical operations performed in the class room, should the teacher know his subject matter in different ways than he does at present?

4. Would the teacher's improved ability to promote the logical handling and exploration of the subject matter make him less dependent on text books?

Answers to these questions are sought on the basis of experiments and if the answers to all these are affirmative that would provide sufficient rationable and justification for instituting special courses in Logic for teachers in the training colleges.

CHAPTER

7

ETHICS OF KNOWLEDGE AND EDUCATION

0.1 THE PRESENT DAY WORLD is passing through a period which is beset with value-crisis. This crisis has pervaded all the spheres of value-realisation, but it is felt much more deeply in the field of education. It is mirrored in the students community in the form of aimlessness, indiscipline, unrest, strikes, violence, disobedience of authority etc. What is needed is to make a philosophical analysis of the problem so as to find out its very roots, and to attempt to visualise whether a reform in education which is the most important and foundational sphere of value-realisation, can bring about its dissolution.

7.1.0 The deeper penetration into the problem would reveal the fact that the present day tendency of value-negativism is a resultant phenomenon of the loss of faith in a moral order. The inevitable consequence of such a circumstance has been the disappearance of moral virtues and the spread of vices. As a matter of fact these two phenomena are the two aspects of the same situation. In order to resolve the value-crisis two ways, to be employed simultaneously, can be suggested. The first is that of cure, i.e., to diagnose the possible causes of the origin of vice. The second is that of prevention, that is to say, to provide morality a solid rational footing. In the present chapter we shall concentrate on the former.[1]

7.2.0 A psychological analysis of the pathological cases will bring home to us as to why vice is due to. There seem to be four main factors which occasion vice, viz., badness, madness, rashness and folly. We may explain each one of these:

(*i*) In some individuals vices are innate and intrinsic. They possess some such psycho-ontological qualities of 'tamas' that they cannot do otherwise except evil. Like Nero they may rejoice in doing evil or, like Duryodhana they may possess the ability to recognise evil as evil and yet may not desist from doing it. They may know the good and yet may lack the will to do it.

(*ii*) In some cases man's evil deeds result from some sort of mental disease. Such people are not bad but only mad. They do not have the discriminative capacity and the power to foresee the consequences.

(*iii*) Some people, who are neither bad nor mad, tend to do evil, not voluntarily, but because they are compelled to do so by the circumstances.

(*iv*) But in the most cases evil is due to ignorance or folly. Socrates has rightly opined that virtue is knowledge and vice is ignorance. The Upaniśads also aver the same, 'Avidyayā mṛtyumāpnoti vidyayā amṛtmaśnute'. The evil

1. I have attempted the latter in my symposium address 'Must Ethics be based on Religion ?' to the 40th session of the Indian Philosophical Congress. See the proceedings of the Indian Philosophical Congress, 1967.

doer does not know the evilness of his act, otherwise he would not have acted that way. So it is the lack of knowledge, and not voluntary sinfulness that issues in bad conduct.

7.2.1 The ratio of the first group is quite negligible and these people can be checked only by constant vigilance and can be deterred by strict punishment. It is difficult to reform them through education or legislation. Those who fall under the second group should be sent to reformatories and treated psychologically. The people coming under the third category can be brought on the track by proper training and by improving their lot. The fourth group, which, as we have said, is the largest one, definitely requires a moral and spiritual training. The last three groups provide the rationale for moral and spiritual instruction.

7.2.2 Here, it may be argued that the sinner knows that it is bad to commit sin and yet he does it. So it is not ignorance but willfulness which is the cause of evil. But in such a view the connotation of knowledge is misconceived. By knowledge we do not mean mere intellectual awareness. It stands for wisdom which consists in a practical sense of values. This is the purport of the poet saint Kabirdas when he laments, "pothī padhi padhi jaga muā pandita bhayā na koya." So a true knowledge must tell upon one's behaviour. There is no gap between genuine knowing and its doing. When the Gita declares that 'yogah karmasu kauśalaṁ,' or, the Mahābhārata asserts that 'yah kriyāvān sa panditah', it is contended that there should be a conjunction of true knowledge and goodwill. One who knows the good cannot stop exercising it. When Duryodhana boasted that he knows the Dharma, his knowledge was only superficial and not genuine. To know the good and not to act upto it is a psychological impossibility. A true knowledge of the good must stir the whole being of man. It must be noetic or illuminating. This is what the Jaina thinkers have declared when they said that *samyak jñāna* inevitably leads to *samyak caritra*. Socrates and Jesus Christ also meant the same when they said that the sinner does not really know what the good is.

From the above it is evident that wisdom or true knowledge is not devoid of action, that it consists in a practical sense of values, and that virtue being knowledge can be taught and acquired. What is needed is to train the individual in a proper way to know the good and to act upto it. And here comes the role of education. This is what is called the educational theory of goodness.

7.3.0 The Indian seers were all the while conscious of this fact that a man devoid of wisdom can never be noble. 'Dhiyā vihīno nahi yati dhanyatāṁ' So the task of education must be to inculcate in him wisdom or a practical sense of values. The words saṃskāra, saṃskṛti, dvija, saṭṭva, saṁshuddhi, viśuddhātmā, nididhyāsan etc. used for education and educated beings suggest the true character of education which was imparted in those days. The famous convocation address in the Taittirīya Upaniśad starts with Satyaṁ Vada, Dharmaṁ-Cara etc. All this emphasises that wisdom can be acquired by him alone who has moral and spiritual qualifications. At present under the western influence we concentrate only on the measures (pramāṇās) of knowledge and do not take into consideration the most significant part played by the measures of knowledge (pramātṛ). The various instruments of knowledge like sound, sense organs, sharp intellect, adequate methodology etc. do play their role in the acquisition of knowledge, but more important is the knower who uses these instruments. The moral and spiritual character of the knower influences his capacity of acquiring the truth. The five-fold gradation of knowledge in the jain epistemology, the sādhanā catuṣtaya of the Advaita Vedānta, the sādhana saptaka of Rāmānuja's philosophy etc. all evince the truth that the greater the purification of being, the more certain is knowledge.

7.4.0 The upshot of the above consideration is that the prime need of the day is a re-orientation of our nature of education. Instead of being mere job-oriented let it also be character-oriented. If our system education fails to turn over a man into a man it has outlived its utility and is more than a dead weight.

APPENDIX

EDUCATION FROM A LOGICAL* POINT OF VIEW

LOGIC CAN BROADLY be defined as the study of the principles and methods of valid reasoning. What interests a logician is the correctness of the process of reasoning. His prime concern here is the connection between the conclusions arrived at and the grounds (or evidence) on which those conclusions are based. There can be three possibilities which can logically be conceived with regard to such a connection. It may be necessary in the sense that the grounds are such that the conclusions derived from them cannot be denied. Or, it may be contingent (*i.e.*, probable) in the sense that the grounds are such that subject to certain qualifications the conclusions based on them can justifiably be asserted. Or, it may be impossible in the sense that the grounds can never entail the conclusion.

There is another function of logic which has of late been recognized and developed. This function of logic can be named as linguistic and conceptual analysis. The significance of this function lies in the fact that all thinking has to find its

* Here the term 'logical' has been used in a very wide sense which comprehends deduction as well as induction and methodology.

expression through a language. But although language is indispensable, it may hinder logicality of thought when it is used emotively. So much hair-splitting can be avoided if the language employed is free from ambiguity, confusion and opacity.

Logical Dimensions of Education

A study in the logical foundations of education would reveal two significant roles which logic could perform (and, therefore, must be called upon to perform) in the sphere of education. They are : (*i*) analysis of the language of educational discourse, and (*ii*) determining the logical components of the educational process.

We any elaborate these two points in some detail.

Logic and the 'Language of Education'

Language, being the medium of expression of thought, must be so transparent as to be able to faithfully represent the thought otherwise, it would fail to serve its intended purpose. The language used by educational researchers and practitioners is not always adequate. Because of its 'open texture', it tends to distort and twist the gist of the subject. It also usually abounds in abbreviations, compressions, ellipses, suppressed premises, misleading metaphors, inadequate analogies, and the like, which conceal or misdirect the very purport. Because of such careless use of language, many assumptions slip in educational discourse which may be in conflict with the general drift of the theory or practice of which the educator may not be aware. For example, how the standard S-R formulation of psychology, when borrowed in education, conceals an assumption unwarranted by the data about the way in which the stimuli act on the organism, is clearly revealed by William W. Rozeboom (1961).

APPENDIX

EDUCATION FROM A LOGICAL* POINT OF VIEW

LOGIC CAN BROADLY be defined as the study of the principles and methods of valid reasoning. What interests a logician is the correctness of the process of reasoning. His prime concern here is the connection between the conclusions arrived at and the grounds (or evidence) on which those conclusions are based. There can be three possibilities which can logically be conceived with regard to such a connection. It may be necessary in the sense that the grounds are such that the conclusions derived from them cannot be denied. Or, it may be contingent (*i.e.*, probable) in the sense that the grounds are such that subject to certain qualifications the conclusions based on them can justifiably be asserted. Or, it may be impossible in the sense that the grounds can never entail the conclusion.

There is another function of logic which has of late been recognized and developed. This function of logic can be named as linguistic and conceptual analysis. The significance of this function lies in the fact that all thinking has to find its

* Here the term 'logical' has been used in a very wide sense which comprehends deduction as well as induction and methodology.

Loose thinking also is very current among the educators. Proverbs, sayings, slogans, etc., are very often used, which are sometimes vague, false or meaningless. For example, when it is said that 'All that glitters is not gold', it does not convey any precise meaning. What an idealist thinker means when he uses it, can be made clear only when it is converted into a directly meaningful sentence. Similarly, some educators are fond of exhorting. 'Teach children and not subjects'. As a slogan it may have some value of emphasis, but when it is taken literally and put in the form of a dilemma, "what do teachers teach? Do they teach subject-matter or do they teach children?" then it becomes a quite ridiculous because we always teach something to somebody.

The analysis of educational language would also make it clear that the language of educating (activity) is not the same as the language of education as a discipline (science). One is the language in which teacher and pupil communicate and the other is the language in which a disciplined knowledge is expressed. The same analysis alone would further enable us to standardize the use of these two types of languages.

Logic and Educational Concepts

Like the educational language, many educational concepts are also quite vague and often misleading. For example, it is maintained that education is a 'process of self-realization'. But what 'self' and 'realization' precisely mean has been often left vague with the result that this concept fails to signify anything concrete. Equally vague and misleading are the phrases like 'education according to nature' or 'education as a process of development of personality and character'. Similarily, phrases like 'meeting the needs of youth', 'providing life experiences' and a host of other ares either too vague to be of practical use or beyond the capacity of the educational institutions to fulfil.

Moreover, educators often use the same concept to denote different objects. Conflicting uses of terms like 'role', 'need', 'status', 'freedom', authority', 'creativity', 'nature', 'development', 'knowing' and the like lead to disagreements about how data are to be collected and classified, and conclusions established. This comes in the way of agreed findings.

It is here again that the role of logical analysis is called for. It can help us : (*i*) in detecting enigmatic, pretentious and tautologous definitions of educational phenomena, and (*ii*) in developing an agreed set of concepts to describe them. Such an analysis can have three phases :

(*a*) Charting out the various possible meanings of a concept.

(*b*) Defining the senses in which it is used in different theories within a single branch of inquiry and also among the different branches of inquiry.

(*c*) Studying implications of their sense in educational theory and codifying their usage.

Such an attempt will bring about unanimity, precision and clarity in educational discourse and thus ensure effective communication which can guarantee mutual understanding, which operates in the realm of natural sciences. As a matter of fact, there have been some significant studies made by the analytic thinkers in this direction. Gilbert Ryle (1959) in 'The Concept of Mind', has clarified many mental-conduct concepts like 'knowing', 'teaching'. 'learning', etc. The concept of 'adjustment' has been analysed by C.J.B. Macmillan (Kneller, 1964). B. Paul Komisar (1961, 1962) has analyed the concept of 'need'. In collaboration with Jerold R. Coombs (1964), he has also worked out different meanings of the concept of 'equality'. B. Othanel Smith and Robert H. Ennis (1961) have done a great service in editing the book entitled, 'Language and Concepts in Education'. In this book, Smith has analysed three meanings of the concept of 'teaching' (pp. 96-101). Israel Scheffler (1960) has worked out the logical implications of two kinds of statements common in educational discourse, viz., statements of definitions and statements of slogans. He has also discussed their respective valid roles and logical force in educational discourse. The work of R.S. Peters (1967) is also a significant advance in this direction.

All these studies are pioneering efforts in this new field and have to be carried further. The imperative need today is the standardization of the concepts used in educational discourse so that they are used scientifically and are employed with discrimination.

Logic and Generalizations in Education

There has been a tendency among the educators and educational researchers to base their theories and practices on generalizations borrowed from the behavioural sciences. But many of these generalizations are based on certain assumptions which are uncritically accepted, and for which there may not be any warrant in experience. This is specially so with regard to the assumptions about human nature in psychology and sociology. For example, Herbart's concept of mind as *tabule rasa* seems to be quite fantastic. Similarly, in psychology, there are many 'schools' and the psychologists interpret the data they study in the light of the teachings of the school to which they owe allegiance. Hence, educational theories and practices based on psychological theories are no more to be trusted than the assumptions of the schools that have provided the theories in question. One of the functions of the logical critique of educational thought should be to examine such assumptions and generalizations.

Logic and Educational Analogies

Educators often draw analogies between certatin educational phenomena and the phenomena in other realms. Analogies are usually drawn out of metaphors. A metaphorical statement indicates important analogies between two phenomena in certain respects without explicitly stating in what the analogies actually consist. The theoretical value of a metaphor lies in the fact that it points out significant parallels and may hint at a successful hypothesis. Thus, it has a serious theoretical role to play.

But analogies are neither deductions nor valid inductive causal inferences, nor a statistical inference in terms of probabilities. And therefore, though they are not always false, they are weak and need to be used cautiously. The metaphors usually suffer from two types of weaknesses. They may prove to be sterile or trivial, like the metaphor of the *tabula rasa* employed by Locke and Herbart, or of organic growth used by Dewey for cultural growth. The second type of weakness is that they may be limited in the sense that their applicability is contextual and that they give only a specific perspective on their subjects. Such a limitation is not a reason to reject them completely. Analogies can be profitably drawn, provided two conditions are kept in mind, namely : (*i*) it is rewarding to give a comparison of alternative metaphors just as alternative theories are rewarding in science in revealing the multifaceted character of the subject ; (*ii*) no attempt should be made to transplant the metaphors since each one is relevant to a particular context only.

Educators generally overlook these conditions and employ indiscriminately the metaphors of the mirror or the lamp to explain the state of mind of the learner, or the metaphors of growth or moulding, or carving to explain the respective roles of teacher and the pupil in the process of education. So, the point in reference is that to call attention to analogies that may control the discussions of educational objectives and means, and to examine their credentials, is a task which a logical critique alone can undertake.

Logic and Educational Inferences

Many educational thinkers and researchers derive conclusions from data which do not usually provide complete grounds for those conclusions. The result is that many statements about educational phenomena are based on faulty inferences and inept value-judgements. For example, it has been very often contended that since the teachers are low paid, the quality of teachers is poor in India. Firstly, the premise itself is disputable that apart, it does not offer any strict logical reason for the conclusion. There is no necessary and invariable connection between low wages and the inferior quality of teachers. To give one more example, the Centre of Advanced Study in Education, M.S. University of Baroda, brought out a report (1967) on our educational standards. The reliability of the method of questionnaire employed in this study apart, the study is vitiated with certain internal flaws. For example, while discussing the tabulated results of the responses to Item No. 1 of the questionnaire (p. 2) 'standard of development in certain habits and interests' (c in the list) is regarded as dichotomous with 'development of attitude' (g in the list). To quote the actual wording of the report: "On the basis of percentage values, a clear-cut dichotomy is seen between a, b, c and d, e, f forming two different groups'. But it is beyond one's comprehension how development of attitude can be contrasted with development of habits and interests in such a way as to admit of dichotomy. Further, Items No. 7 and 8, as well as 10 and 11 seem to overlap with each other, and violate the rule of parsimony. Implicit in the garb of a positive language these items contain many negative suggestions which should have been avoided in order to elicit spontaneous responses.

A critical analysis of most of such reports would bring out an array of logical flaws of which the writers might not be aware. So, if the researcher is given some training in the technique of logical thinking, he would perhaps be able to avoid such fallacious reasoning. A training in logic would not only help him in the selection of appropriate set of evidences and in the derivation of legitimate conclusions from it, but it would also provide him with a valid and suitable methodology for solving problems and tackling issues. This will be done by pointing out the nature and steps involved in different research methodologies, and the limitations and the range of phenomena they cover.

Logic and Theory Construction in Educational Research

In the discipline of education, there are many low-level generalizations rather than scientifically tested theories. It has been contended that these generalizations often mislead the educator and cause great harm to the theory and practice of education. In order to avoid such generalizations, techniques of science are brought into the field of education. But ere we apply these techniques of science to the problem of education, we should be well-trained in the process of 'construct validation' so that the methods of theory construction used by us may not be poor or fallacious and hence of negative validity or low reliability. Lest our remedial measures harbour newer vices, it is imperative that we should make a studied use of the scientific methods by duly taking into consideration the logical principles involved in them. For example, the Hempelian model for explanation is based on four logical principles which must invariably be followed. They are: (*a*) the explanandum must be a logical consequence of the explanans, (*b*) the explanans must contain general laws required for the derivation of the explanandum, (*c*) the explanans must have empirical content, and (*d*) the sentences constituting the explanans must be true.

What is needed, then, is that educational researchers should also be trained in the discipline of logical analysis.

Logic and Educational Measurements

Just as for theory-construction the methods of science have been introduced in the field of education, in the same way scientific measuring devices and tests have also been brought in. For example. in order to judge intelligence educational measurements have been constructed on the imitation of the measurements in physics. It is very much doubtful whether we can measure the properties of the intelligence in the same way in which we measure physical properties. Further, all these measurement tests evolved by educational psychologists are based on behaviouristic presuppositions, whose roots lie in the physics which has long ago been discarded. Still, without doubting the futility of these mental measurement tests, as they are called, it can be asked that out of the three senses of measurement which occur in physics, viz., intensive magnitudes, fundamental magnitudes and derived magnitudes, in which sense are the properties measured in educational experiments? There does not appear to be general agreement among educationists as to the answer to this question. But upon the answer to this alone depends the genuineness of the devices employed, because the logical principles underlying the three types of measurements are not the same.

Logic and Educational Curricula

There is another sphere of education, viz., curriculum-framing, where the help of logic must be sought. The focal point of all educational phenomena ultimately centres round the teaching-learning process. But the character and outcome of this process depends on the curriculum and methods that are employed; and the latter, in turn, are dependent upon the way in which they stand in relation to knowledge. Knowledge is thus the very stock, so to say, in the trade of education.

Now, in order that the teaching-learning process may be smooth and interesting, it is necessary to arrange the instructional material in a logical way. Under the zeal to psychologize everything mental, it has been falsely believed that mind is a logical and that logical order is detrimental to interest and motivation. The fact, however, is that logical order is rather conducive to the development of interest. Moreover, it is fallacious to believe that the logical order and the psychological order are antithetical and hence do not go hand in hand. The logical order is never rigidly fixed and stereotyped. On the contrary, the logical arrangement of the knowledge, though peculiar to each individual discipline, nevertheless is quite amenable to the stage of development reached by the learner. The process of such an arrangement is from simple to complex, but 'simple' and 'complex' are relative notions depending upon the mental development of the learner. Thus through a psychological approach, the logical organization is reached; and, in this way, the organization is simultaneously both logical as well as psychological.

Logic and Educational Methods of Assessment

Assessment plays a key role in judging the outcome of the process of education. Through it alone we fathom the effectiveness of teaching and the depth of learning. The usual method employed for this task is that of setting a question paper. But to ask a question is not the same as to ask the right question. Many of our question papers set in the examinations suffer from inherent flaws, some of which can be enumerated here:

1. Depending on the source of information, some questions for their answer depend on investigation and some call for introspection. Questions pertaining to the facts of sense experience which are empirically testable, fall under the first category, whereas questions like 'Are our wills free?' require only reflexion. So, while expecting the response from the pupils, this distinction should not be overlooked.

2. With regard to the answerability; some questions are answerable in principle but may not be so in practice, either nor or ever. Questions like the number of hair on the head, etc., are such and care should be taken by the examiner to avoid such questions.

3. On the basis of the motive of the questioner, a distinction must be made between 'fact-finding' and 'verbal' questions. For example, if some one committed a particular act and the

jury were asked to opine whether it was legal or illegal, this question would not demand any fact-finding but only interpretation of the wording of the law or principle.

4. In most of the question papers, we find a question pertaining to definitions and pupils are asked to state whether a particular definition is true or false. But definitions are of two types, viz., biverbal, and ostensive. It should be remembered that truth value belongs to the former type only.

5. There are certain structural fallacies in the framing up of the questions and care must be taken to avoid them.

Loaded questions like "Do you approve the act of Mr. X?", or "Don't you like him?" clearly hint at the kind of answer demanded. Closed, questions like, "Who will win, X or Y?", shut out the possibilities of further selection if the alternatives are more than two. Some questions embody built-in-assumptions like, "Have you stopped stealing?". Questions like, "Who is your favourite hero?", suffer from question-begging when one has no such particular choice. In some questions, there is built-in-unanswerability, e.g. in philosophy, if it is asked, "How is the world related to the Absolute?", then the question would be non-sensical since Absolute, by definition, is one who is beyond all relations.

These and many more such flaws can be detected and avoided, provided a logical analysis is undertaken.

LOGIC AND THE TEACHING-LEARNING PROCESS

Lastly, logic provides the very basis of the teaching-learning process. Since the aim of all education is to communicate knowledge effectively, the success of teacher-learning strategy lies in fulfilling two conditions. They are:

1. When its key words like teaching, learning, expounding,

explaining, defining, justifying, etc., are adequately defined and properly used.

2. When the sentences in which the ideas or thoughts are presented are systematically linked with one another. This is necessary because in this process we begin somewhere and end somewhere. Neither is the beginning at random nor is the end abrupt. From a set of premises, a reasoned discourse leads to conclusion. It is, therefore, logical.

In the present-day curricula, we have neglected the role of language and discarded the role of logic. Those who disregard logic in education suffer from the erroneous notion that the principles of logic deal only with the ideal thinking process and they have nothing to do with the actual thinking process. But the fact is that these principles are helpful in scanning our thinking. They tell us whether or not the conclusions we have reached follow necessarily from our premises, or, as in inductive thinking, they decide the probable truth of our conclusions. Moreover, those who try to move directly from the psychologists' description of how men learn to a position on how men ought to learn, and try to derive educational method from a psychology of learning are showing a basic fallacy of judgement. There can be no justified leap from that which is descriptive to that which is prescriptive. The emphasis upon psychology and the relative absence of logical studies in the curricula of teacher-training institutions furnish primary evidence that we have fallen into this error.

Conclusion

From the above considerations, it is quite clear that logic can be highly useful in the field of educational research and training. It can help to raise the standards of educational research by analysing the logical structure of the presented knowledge, by reconstructing the language of educational discourse and by proposing canons of theory and concept formation. The method of logical analysis is also remarkably congenial to the problems of education. It clarifies concepts and assumptions, unsnarls logical and linguistic tangles in pedagogical knowledge, states criteria for meaning, explanation and verification and provides models of theory. Logic is also an inherent element in the teacher-learning process and an understanding of the logical operations involved in it makes the task of the teacher and pupil more orderly and effective.

BIBLIOGRAPHY

Archambault, R.D. (Ed.). *Philosophical Analysis and Education.* New York: Humanities Press, 1965.

Ascher, M.J. *The Analysis of Classroom Discourse.* (Ph.D. Thesis). University of Illinois, 1959.

Banghart, F.W. (Ed.). *First Annual Phi Delt a Kappa Symposium on Educational Research.* Bloomington: Indiana, Phi Delta Kappa, 1960.

Berlak, H. The teaching of thinking. *The School Review*, Spring 1965, 70 (3).

Brubacher, John, S. *Modern Philosophies of Education*, McGraw-Hill, New York, 1950.

Bruce, J., Biddle and William J. Elleme (Eds.). *Contemporary Research on Teacher Effectiveness.* New York: Holt, Rinehart and Winston, 1964.

Bruner, J.S. *The Process of Education.* Combridge: Harvard University Press, 1961.

——— *Studies in Cognitive Growth.* New York: Wiley, 1966.

——— Study of thinking. *Science Editore.* New York, 1962.

——— *Towards a Theory of Instruction.* Cambridge: Belknap Press of Harvard University, 1966.

Burns, H.W. and Brauner, C.J. *Philosophy of Education.* New York: Ronald Press, 1962.

Butler, J. Donald, *Four Philosophies and Their Practices on Education and Religion*, Harper, New York, 1957.

Broudy, H.S. *Building a Philosophy of Education*, Prentice-Hall, Englewood, Cliffs, N.J. 1954.

Ennis, R.H. A concept of critical thinking. *Harvard Educational Review*, Winter 1962, 32.

Feigl Herbart and Grover Maxwell. *Current Issues in Philosophy of Science*. New York; Holt, Rinehart and Winston, 1961.

——— and Michael Scriven. (Eds.). *Minnesota Studies in the Philosophy of Science*, Vols. 1, 2 and 3. Minnaepolis: University of Minnesota Press, 1956.

——— and May Brodbeck. *Readings in the Philosophy of Science*. New York: Appleton Century-Crofts, 1953.

Ford, G.W. and Lawrence, P. *The Structure of Knowledge and the Curriculum*. Chicago: Rand McNally, 1964.

Gage, N.L. *Handbook of Research on Teaching*. Chicago: Rand McNally, 1963.

Hardie, C.D. *Truth and Fallacy in Educational Theory*. Cambridge University Press, 1942.

Henry Nelson, B. ed. *The Forty-first Year book of the National Society for the Study of Education*, Vol. I., University of Chicago, Chicago, 1955.

Inhelder, B. and Piget, J. *The Growth of Logical Thinking*. London: Routledge and Kegan Paul, 1958.

Israel Scheffler. (Ed.). *Philosophy and Education*. Boston: Allyn and Bacon, 1958.

——— *The Language of Education*. Illinois: Thomas, Springfield, 1960.

——— *Conditions of Knowledge*. Chicago: Scott, Foresman, 1965.

Judges, A.V. Ed. *Education and the Philosophic Mind*, Harrap, London, 1957.

Kneller, G.F., ed., *Foundations of Education*, John Wiley, New York, 1963.

Kneller, G.F., *Logic and Language of Education*, John Wiley, New York, 1966.

——— *Logic and Language of Education*. New York: Wiley, 1964.

Komisar B. Paul. *Needs and the needs-curriculum.* In Smith, B.O. and Ennis, R.H. (Eds.). Language and Concepts in Education. Chicago: Rand McNally, 1966.

——— and Coombs, J.R. *The concept of equality in education.* Studies in Philosophy and Education. Fall, 1964.

———*Introduction to Philosophy of the Education.* New York: Wiley, 1964.

Michael Scriven. The Philosophy of science in educational research. *Review of Educational Research,* December 1960, 30.

Maccia Elizabeth. Logic of education and of educatology. In Black, H.C. (Ed.). *Proceedings of the 20th Annual Meeting of the Philosophy of Education Society,* University of Kansas, 1964.

Macmillan, C.J.B. Equality and sameness. *Studies in Philosophy and Education,* Winter 1964-65, 3.

Nash Paul. *Authority and Freedom in Education.* New York: Wiley, 1966.

O'Connor, D.J. *Introduction to the Philosophy of Educator,* London: Routledge and Kegan Paul, 1957.

Peters, R.S. *The Concept of Education.* London: Routledge and Kegan Paul, 1967.

Park Joe, ed. *Selected Readings in the Philosophy of Education,* Macmillan, New York, 1958.

Phenix, Philips, H. *Philosophy of Education,* Holt, Rinehat, Winston, New York, 1958.

Ross, J.S. *Ground Work of Educational Theory.* George G. Harrap, London, 1964 ed.

Rozeboom, W.W. Formal analysis and the language of behavioural theory. In Herbart Feigal and Grover Maxwell. (Eds.). *Current Issues in Philosophy of Science, op. cit.*

Rusk, R.R. *The Philosophical Base of Education.* University of London, 1956 ed.

Smith, B.O. and Repart, H. Ennis (Eds.). *Language and Concepts in Education.* Chicago: Rand McNally, 1966.

—— et e. A Study of the logic of teaching *First and Second Reports of the S.U. Office of Education.* Bureau of Educational Research. Urbana: University of Illinois, 1959, 1964.

Ulich, Robert. *Philosophy of Education.* American Book Company, New York, 1961.

Weber, C.O. *Basic Philosophies of Education.* Rinehart, New York, 1960.

INDEX